# *Tove Jansson*

**Twayne's World Authors Series**

Scandinavian Literature

**Leif Sjöberg, Editor**
*State University of New York, Stony Brook*

TOVE JANSSON
(1914–   )
Photograph by Per Olov Jansson

# Tove Jansson

## By W. Glyn Jones

### The University of Newcastle upon Tyne

*Twayne Publishers · Boston*

*Tove Jansson*

W. Glyn Jones

Copyright © 1984 by G.K. Hall & Company
All Rights Reserved
Published by Twayne Publishers
A Division of G. K. Hall & Company
70 Lincoln Street
Boston, Massachusetts 02111

Printed on permanent/durable
acid-free paper and bound in the
United States of America.

**Library of Congress Cataloging in Publication Data**

Jones, W. Glyn.
Tove Jansson.

(Twayne's world authors series; TWAS 716.
Finland)
Bibliography: p.
Includes index.
1. Jansson, Tove—Criticism and interpretation.
I. Title. II. Series: Twayne's world authors
series; TWAS 716. III. Series: Twayne's world
authors series. Finland.
PT9875.J37Z74   1984   839.7'374   83-12413
ISBN 0-8057-6563-8

## Contents

About the Author

Preface

Chronology

> CHAPTER ONE
> Background, Ideas, and Influences     1
>
> CHAPTER TWO
> The Little Trolls and the Great Flood     14
>
> CHAPTER THREE
> Comet in Moominland and The Comet Is Coming     19
>
> CHAPTER FOUR
> Finn Family Moomintroll     26
>
> CHAPTER FIVE
> The Exploits of Moominpappa     38
>
> CHAPTER SIX
> Moominsummer Madness     48
>
> CHAPTER SEVEN
> Moominland Midwinter     56
>
> CHAPTER EIGHT
> Tales from Moomin Valley     67
>
> CHAPTER NINE
> Moominpappa at Sea     79
>
> CHAPTER TEN
> Moominvalley in November     93
>
> CHAPTER ELEVEN
> The Sculptor's Daughter     106

CHAPTER TWELVE
The Listener    117

CHAPTER THIRTEEN
The Summer Book    127

CHAPTER FOURTEEN
Sun City    138

CHAPTER FIFTEEN
The Doll's House    149

CHAPTER SIXTEEN
Conclusion    163

List of English Names with Swedish Equivalents    167

Notes and References    169

Selected Bibliography    172

Index    175

## *About the Author*

Glyn Jones was appointed to the Queen Alexandra Lectureship in Danish in University College London in 1956. Ten years later he became Reader in Danish in the University of London, and in 1973 was appointed to the first Chair of Scandinavian Studies in Newcastle upon Tyne. He was Visiting Professor of Danish in the University of Iceland in 1971 and Professor of Literature in the Faroese Academy 1979-81. He has lectured widely in Great Britain and on the Continent of Europe. He is the British member of the Editorial Board of Books from Finland and a member of the Advisory Editorial Board of Scandinavica. Since 1976 he has been a member of the Danish-British Cultural Commission and is a corresponding member of the Swedish Literature Society in Finland.

Professor Jones's special interest has been late nineteenth- and twentieth-century literature. His first major publication was a study in Danish of the mature work of the Danish poet and hagiographer Johannes Jørgensen. This was followed in 1969 by a full-length study of the same poet for the Twayne series. In 1970 came a history of Denmark in the Benn/Praeger series of Nations of the Modern World, and in 1974 his two books on the Faroese author William Heinesen, first in the Twayne series, and then in an adapted and expanded version in Danish under the title Færø og kosmos. With his appointment to Newcastle, Professor Jones began to take a serious interest in the Swedish-language literature of Finland, a subject in which his Department now specializes. The present volume on Tove Jansson is a direct result of this interest. Together with his wife, Kirsten Gade, Professor Jones has written a Danish Grammar, published in Copenhagen in 1981. Apart from these major publications he has written extensively on the literature of Denmark, Finland, and the Faroe Islands.

## *Preface*

Tove Jansson's literary and artistic output has been extensive, comprising not only the Moomin books, but also books for adults, strip cartoons, children's picture books, television and radio plays, and countless drawings and illustrations. Something, therefore, had to be excluded from this book. The choice was not difficult, however, for Tove Jansson's literary reputation is based on her prose works, and it is these I have chosen to deal with.

The method has been to let the books speak for themselves, tracing through them the line of development over some forty years. In doing this I have been able to dispense with extensive footnotes, though I have indicated where to find all quotations in the original Swedish as well as in English.

Tove Jansson's books about the Moomintrolls have been, with the exception of the first and the revised version of the second, all translated into English. These translations have become part of English lore. For this reason, I have chosen to quote from the standard translations and to use the names accorded to the various characters in the English versions. The original Swedish names are then listed at the end of the book, together with their English counterparts.

This study was written during a two-year period spent in the Faroe Islands, and I would like to express my appreciation to the Faroese Academy for allowing me to use its facilities. Also, I wish to thank the staff of the Faroese National Library, Føroya Landsbókasavn, for their ever-ready help, and the members of the Finnish Literature Information Centre for their advice. Not least, my thanks go to the British Academy for a grant to visit Finland in 1978 to begin work on the project.

W. Glyn Jones

The University of Newcastle upon Tyne

# *Chronology*

| | |
|---|---|
| 1914 | Tove Marika Jansson born 9 August, eldest child of Viktor Jansson (1886-1958) and Signe Hammarsten Jansson (1882-1970). |
| 1930-1933 | Studies art at Tekniska Konsthantverksskolan, Stockholm. |
| 1933 | Studies at Ateneum, the Finnish Society's school of drawing and painting. |
| 1934 | Two months' study in Germany. |
| 1945 | The Little Trolls and the Great Flood. |
| 1946 | Comet in Moominland. |
| 1947-1948 | Moomintroll series in Ny Tid. |
| 1948 | Studies in Brittany. Publishes Finn Family Moomintroll. |
| 1949 | Studies in Italy. |
| 1950 | The Exploits of Moominpappa. |
| 1952 | Awarded Svenska Dagbladet's Literary Prize. |
| 1953 | Studies in London. |
| 1954 | Moomintroll series starts in London Evening News. Publishes Moominsummer Madness. |
| 1957 | Moominland Midwinter. |
| 1958 | Awarded prize by Swedish Literature Society in Finland. |

TOVE JANSSON

| | |
|---|---|
| 1961 | Appointed to Committee of Fund for Swedish Artists and Musicians. |
| 1962 | <u>Tales from Moomin Valley</u>. |
| 1965 | <u>Moominpappa at Sea</u>. |
| 1966 | Awarded the Hans Christian Andersen Medal. |
| 1968 | <u>The Comet Is Coming</u> and <u>The Sculptor's Daughter</u>. |
| 1969-1973 | Serves on board of Finnish Authors' Society. |
| 1971 | Awarded Tolland Prize by Swedish Literature Society in Finland. Publishes <u>The Listener</u>. |
| 1972 | <u>The Summer Book</u> and <u>Moominvalley in November</u>. |
| 1973 | Awarded prize by the Swedish Academy. |
| 1974 | <u>Sun City</u>. |
| 1976 | Awarded Polish <u>Order of the Smile</u>. |
| 1977 | Awarded annual prize of the Society for the Promotion of Swedish Literature. |
| 1978 | Awarded the Topelius Prize. Created Honorary Doctor at Åbo Academy. Publishes <u>The Doll's House</u>. |
| 1980 | Awarded "Dunce's Hat" by the Finnish Comic Strip Society (together with her brother, Lars Jansson). |

*Chapter One*
# Background, Ideas, and Influences

The twentieth century has seen the emergence in Scandinavia of two children's writers, Tove Jansson and Astrid Lindgren, whose names have become household words throughout the world. They have both at an early stage created their own fantasy worlds, different as they are, centered in the one instance on the Moomin family and in the other on Pippi Longstocking, the first quiet, gentle, romantic at times, the other boisterous and full of fun. Both writers have, after creating their own fantasy worlds, felt the necessity to explore other fields. Astrid Lindgren has kept, broadly speaking, within the field of children's stories, though they reflect a vast register of mood and genre, whereas Tove Jansson has moved further and further away from the children's story into the realm of adult literature--which nevertheless has themes and motifs in common with her earlier work. Meanwhile, within the earlier creations, parallels have been sought and drawn between these two outstanding authors. Writing in the Danish newspaper Information in 1966, Ulla-Stina Nilsson argued that "Moomintroll becomes a dream figure in just the same way as Pippi Longstocking, whose great popularity without doubt can be ascribed to the fact that she is a girl doing just what she wants to do--and what we probably want to do but do not dare" (1).

This article was written on the occasion of Tove Jansson's being awarded the Hans Christian Andersen Medal, "the greatest distinction which can be made to a children's author." It was only one of the many awards and prizes she won. Her books have been translated into twenty-five languages, and she receives some fifteen hundred letters a year from enthusiastic devotees all over the world. The story goes that after publishing her picture book Who Shall Comfort Toffle?, Tove Jansson received a letter from an English child who wrote that he would send four pence a week to her to help comfort Toffle, and then he changed the sum

1

to six pence. A slightly different version of this story is found in Ebba Elfving's article in Hufvudstadsbladet of 9 July 1976, in which the child in question is an American boy who at first promises five cents a year and then alters his offer to a once and for all payment of twenty-five cents!

The secret of Tove Jansson's remarkable popularity is not hard to learn. Her Moomin family represents what has been called a "liberal humanism," a slightly confused, tolerant, semi-Bohemian attitude to life that has been compared to the philosophy of Henry Miller or Jacques Tati, an opposition to the conformism that seems irrevocably to follow in the wake of commercialism and technical progress (2). The Moomin world is a fantasy world, an escapist paradise even, but one that attracts children and adults alike because of the security it ultimately offers, even if that security is subject to outside threats and dangers. As early as spring 1963, Frederic and Boel Fleischer viewed Tove Jansson's world in this way in an article in the American Scandinavian Review:

> . . . Tove Jansson's stories and illustrations caught on quickly, and a number of critics have already called them "Classics." At times one wonders whether somewhat older readers are not more moved and fascinated by the soft and sensitive illusions, the soap-bubble dreams of the individualistic characters who inhabit Moomin Valley, which is untouched by the modern age; when the characters' illusions burst they quickly develop new ones. Children are more fascinated by the Moomin family's adventures, their battle for survival against storms, floods, and other natural disasters, and the sudden appearance of frightening beasts. In Tove Jansson's works kindness always wins out over meanness, which children often accept as rather natural and adults tend to regard as wish-fulfilled illusion. In Moomin Valley the idealists and optimists are never defeated. (3)

Any philosophy to be found in the Moomin books seems to have been fortuitous, and Tove Jansson denies seeking to educate her readers: "I make no conscious effort to educate. I do not try to put over any particular view, least of all any 'philosophy.' I try to

describe what fascinates and frightens me, what I see
and remember, and I let it all take place around a
family whose main characteristics are perhaps a kindly
confusion, acceptance of the world around it and the
very unusual way in which its members get on with each
other" (4). In this same discussion with Bo Carpelan,
Tove Jansson touches on the accusation that she is an
escapist. In answer to the suggestion that Moomin
Valley is a paradise for escapists, she replies:

> To be honest, isn't escapism an integral part of
> writing for children? At least it is with me.
> Let's put it this way: if I don't write to amuse or
> educate little children, I must presumably be writ-
> ing for my own childish qualities. Either those I
> have lost or those I can't fit into an adult soci-
> ety, a rather discreet kind of escapism. (5)

The theme is taken up again in an unpublished manuscript:

> Escapism, why not? . . . I know that it is supposed
> to be dreadfully negative. I suppose I am an
> escapist. I have enclosed a family in a valley
> paradise, surrounded them with lofty mountains on
> all sides and only given them a narrow outlet to the
> sea--which of course is itself an escapist symbol.
> Perhaps the excuse is that I am writing children's
> books--for surely children have the right to escape.

However, she adds that her books are written less for
children than for herself, a significant comment, which
may well be an indication of the forces that have led
her away from children's books and turned her into a
highly individual adult author (6).

No author is born in a cultural or historical or
national vacuum, and for some, a knowledge of the
influences--cultural and social--brought to bear on
them throughout their lives is important, even necessary, if their work is to be properly understood. Tove
Jansson, however, is one of those who have the quality
of timelessness; for her the Finnish national and
cultural background certainly makes its impact, but it
is of secondary importance in understanding her writing. The countless thousands of children the world
over who read the Moomin books scarcely wonder about

cultural backgrounds: they find themes of a timeless nature and with a universal appeal, and the character types must surely be recognizable whatever the background of the reader.

As for the significance of Tove Jansson's own life and background, interviews with her and articles about her, her childhood, or her life on the island to which she repairs in the summer all show clearly that there is a direct connection between what she writes in her books and what she has experienced. She has also admitted that people have often seen aspects of themselves in her characters, though she maintains that only two of the figures in the Moomin books are actual portraits: Moominmamma is based on her own mother and Too-ticky on the artist Tuulikki Pietilä. Apart from this, Tove Jansson is reticent about relating her life to her work, and published articles and interviews tend to be imprecise when it comes to details of her non-literary life.

Suffice it, then, to say that Tove Jansson belongs to the Swedish-speaking minority in Finland. She was born of a Swedish mother and a Finland-Swedish father and brought up against the solidly middle-class background that the Swedish-speaking Finns of Helsinki represented; her own artistically minded parents, however, were less inclined to conform to the norms laid down by the respectable middle classes than were many other Finland Swedes. The obvious contrast between the narrow respectability of certain members of this class and the more relaxed attitude of her own immediate surroundings is doubtlessly responsible for some of the contrasts portrayed in her books between, for instance, the fillyjonks and hemulens on the one hand and the Moomin family on the other.

Modest as her background might have been, the home was middle class, and this is reflected in all Tove Jansson's work. Like many Finland-Swedes—indeed like many Finns in general—the family did move out of town and spend the summer months in the country or—in their case—on an island in the archipelago, where they occupied a cabin. The similarity has been pointed out between the Finland-Swedish ritual of closing down the summer residence for the winter and reopening and refurbishing it the following spring, and the way in which the Moomins close down their house to hibernate:

> Life in summer residences in Finland was a very Finland-Swedish phenomenon. It was a way of life for fairly well-to-do and well-established people, and right up to the first world war it was the Swedish speakers who dominated the establishment.
>
> And I (with my roots in that class) recognised Tove Jansson's playful portrayal of the middle class pattern which is so effortlessly merged with a Bohemian way of life. A traditional way of living, and yet with its unconventional features. (7)

Even the architecture of some of these Finnish summer residences, with their towers and romantic roofs, is reminiscent of the Moomin house--though that is supposed to have been inspired by an old-fashioned stove. The mixture of the petit bourgeois and the Bohemian is also pointed out by Lennart Utterström, who emphasizes that the Moomin family--and mutatis mutandi Tove Jansson's own family?--seldom consciously breaks with accepted concepts and conventions (8).

There are in Tove Jansson's work occasional glimpses of rather bedraggled and woebegone creatures, but in general the surroundings reflect a certain standard of life, and her illustrations all represent sizable houses. The same holds true of the adult books: there are very few glimpses of the working classes in them, and whether the action takes place in Tove Jansson's native Helsinki or, occasionally, abroad, the solid middle classes usually assert themselves. There is no sign of social conflict and only here and there, of what could be called social awareness.

There is, however, a constantly recurring motif of security that is threatened from outside. It is not possible to explain this fully, though various reasons for the sense of lurking danger might be pointed out. While Tove was still a very small child, Finland underwent a bloody civil war between the Reds--the communists--and the Whites--the conservative forces--and it may well be that this left traces. Or perhaps the sense of belonging to a minority of 11 percent in a country where the majority was becoming increasingly influential played a part. Or perhaps it can be ascribed to the general sense of insecurity caused by events abroad as well as at home.

Tove Jansson herself makes no direct allusion to any of this in her work, and she has vehemently denied any political parallels, such as those that have been suggested in the conflict between the red spiders and the white hattifatteners in the short story, "The Secret of the Hattifatteners." She does, however, accept that the general situation in which she has been brought up has left its mark on her work:

> Why not? It is a Finland-Swedish family I have described. And there may be traces of the isolation which is inevitably present in any minority. But it is done absolutely without pathos. They are content with each other, with their surroundings and the place in which they live. But of course they must have recognisable Finland-Swedish characteristics-- that isn't intended to be either a good or a bad thing. It's simply how it is. (9)

Tove Jansson's family was "different" in Finland because on the one hand it was Swedish speaking--though this would scarcely be felt in the Swedish-speaking enclave--and on the other because it was a family of artists which maintained a strong artistic tradition with all this meant for the family's life-style. Her mother, the daughter of a Swedish clergyman, was Signe Hammersten Jansson, known by the pseudonym of Ham; she was first and foremost a highly gifted caricaturist, but she was also responsible for the design of many of Finland's banknotes and about two hundred Finnish stamps as well as a large number of book covers, illustrations, and maps. She was, according to all accounts, a practical woman who managed to combine her artistic activities with caring for her husband and three children as well as running a home and a cabin (10). She used to tell stories to her children, and Tove Jansson acknowledges her debt to her for this and for the feeling of comfort and security she experienced as her mother sat near the stove in the dark studio.

Her father was the sculptor Viktor Jansson, known to his friends as Faffan. His artistic creations, some of which are seen on the dust cover of the autobiographical <u>The Sculptor's Daughter</u>, set their stamp on the home. Tove Jansson says that she has powerful visual memories of her childhood home:

> I saw that studio much later, when other artists had been living in it and stamped it with their personalities. I saw how tiny it was, and how changed. But

that did not spoil my original picture of the studio, big and mysterious with a fire in the stove, the shadows and the sculptures. Since then I have felt that any home without sculptures is empty. (11)

According to the author herself, both her parents were active in the Finnish Civil War in 1918, and her father in particular was of a very patriotic disposition. (One remembers Moominpappa, who on one occasion declares himself to be a staunch royalist.) Tove was the eldest of three children (her first brother, Per Olov, was born in 1920 and the second, Lars, in 1926), and she has emphasized that her childhood was a happy one despite uncertain financial circumstances. The members of the family were devoted to one another, but Tove felt herself particularly close to her mother. She has already been acknowledged as the model for Moominmamma, and the question will inevitably arise as to whether Viktor Jansson was the model for Moominpappa. The answer seems to be rather that certain of his characteristics have been borrowed, though Moominpappa falls short of being a re-creation of the author's father.
One aspect of Tove Jansson's work that strikes the reader is her love of islands and her fascination with storms. It seems that her father was at least in part responsible for this.

In the summer [my parents] rented a fisherman's cottage on an island in the eastern part of the Finnish archipelago; it was wild and beautiful and uninhabited. Every time there was a storm Father would take us out in the boat--he loved storms. We sailed to islets which were even wilder and more isolated, and spent the night under the sail during thunderstorms which were far more violent and dangerous than they are now; the waterspouts were higher, and when you got lost in the mushroom woods the autumn darkness was blacker.
We used to save shipwrecked smugglers. Father could waken us in the middle of the night to put out forest fires miles away from our island, and when the water began to rise he was delighted and said: I fear the worst.
But it was Mother who then lit the lamp in the evening. (12)

There is hardly a word in the account that cannot be directly related to the Moomin books and <u>The Sculptor's Daughter</u>, a demonstration beyond doubt of the close relationship between Tove Jansson's own experience and the poeticized reality of the Moomin world.

Tove Jansson has continued the family tradition of retiring to an island, and she comments on this in an unpublished manuscript, in which she uses Moominpappa's island as her point of departure:

> That lonely island in the sea? Well, it was perhaps created less because I didn't like people than because I did like the sea. And if I am now moving out to an even smaller island out in the Finnish archipelago, it is because I have grown even fonder of the sea.

Tove Jansson's cottage "reminds one of an old-fashioned fisherman's cottage or pilot's house, a perfectly ordinary house with four windows, rag rugs, a rocking chair and so on. Even an ornate iron stove which it was difficult to find now that everything is black or white and artistically designed. In this cottage Tove works, writes, illustrates, paints" (13). In another article, the same writer points out that Tove Jansson has done all the planning work on the island, which explains the obvious technical knowledge she exhibits in <u>Moominpappa at Sea</u>, with its glimpses of Pappa in his workshop and building breakwaters on his island.

Tove Jansson at an early age revealed her artistic propensities, and at the age of fifteen, after nine years at school, she went to study art in Stockholm, Helsinki, and Paris. She recalls that her father would not allow her to become a sculptor--but it is apparent that painting was the art form to which she was most attracted from the start.

> My father was a sculptor, but he would never let us touch clay. He said it was enough with one sculptor, I think he tried to protect us. Well, then, I started as a painter and illustrator, and as a young woman I did a lot of illustrations for periodicals and newspapers. I designed book covers, anything at all; no one would buy my paintings, so I managed on illustrations. Later, I only illustrated my own

## Background, Ideas, and Influences

books, but recently I have had some really interesting other jobs. I did them for Bonniers' Swedish versions of <u>Alice in Wonderland</u> and <u>The Hunting of the Snark</u>, and it was great fun, though very difficult. (14)

The principles guiding her in her illustrations are indicated by her in an article in <u>Mediernas värld</u>.

> To illustrate a children's book gives me a feeling of being an intruder in alien territory. I only draw in order to make things clearer, to emphasise or to tone down. The illustrations are nothing but a note in the margin, an attempt to be "considerate." What is too frightening can be modified by a picture, what is not plain can be given a clear outline, a happy moment can be captured and prolonged. (15)

In view of the intimate relationship between illustration and text in the Moomin books (there are no illustrations to Tove Jansson's adult work with the sole exception of a late edition of <u>The Summer Book</u>), it is interesting to note the indication in the first of the above quotations that it is difficult to illustrate the work of others. Tove Jansson herself feels a natural affinity between her illustrations and her text, and she realizes that illustrating her own text means the elimination of possible differences of interpretation between writer and illustrator.

The artists to whom she says she owes the greatest debt are the Impressionists, but she also mentions John Bauer (16) (to whom she devotes some discussion in <u>The Sculptor's Daughter</u>), Arosenius (17), and Elsa Beskow (18). A later interest has been old engravings, "those very intricate ones with masses of detail and mysterious landscapes and volcanoes in eruption." It may well be that these engravings have had their influence on some of her later illustrations, such as those in <u>Moominpappa at Sea</u>.

Tove Jansson has often been asked how she originally thought of the Moomintrolls. The inspiration for their shape at least appears to have come almost by chance.

> The story may sound like an afterthought, but it is really true. In our house hidden away in the Fin-

nish archipelago we used to write things upon the walls. One summer a lengthy discussion developed along the walls. It all started when my brother, Per Olov, jotted down a quasi-philosophical statement and I tried to refute it, and our dispute continued daily. Finally, Per Olov quoted Kant, and the controversy came to an immediate end as this was irrefutable. In annoyance, I drew something that was intended to be extremely ugly, something that resembled a Moomin. So, in a way, Immanuel Kant inspired the first Moomin. (20)

Although it had been her original intention to concentrate exclusively on painting, in 1938 she turned to writing. Her first book, The Little Trolls and the Great Flood--"a rather peculiar story for children that was sold in soft drink stands in Stockholm" (21)-- was then published in Helsinki in 1945 and subsequently in Stockholm; from then onward the children's books took shape. In the mid-1940s, she began experimenting with strip cartoons in the Swedish-language paper Ny Tid, but it was not until 1954 that she made an international name for herself in this field with the Moomintroll cartoons which appeared in the London Evening News and were then syndicated all over the world in forty countries (22). She continued this series for many years, gradually working on it with her brother Lars (Lasse) and finally leaving it entirely to him. She comments on this period of her life:

> At first, when it was new to me, it was fun to work with strips. It was a new medium of expression. . . . After a while I found myself in a dreadful hunt for subjects, which is the curse of all comic strip writers. I had all the faces of the characters staring at me constantly and everywhere I went. (23)

This experience had its literary expression in the short story for adults, "The Strip Cartoon Artist," from The Doll's House.

According to an article in Hufvudstadsbladet, 9 April 1971, Tove Jansson was driven almost to despair over the demands made on her by her strip cartoon work. In the 1950s she had met the artist Tuulikki Pietilä, who "taught her to take a more relaxed attitude to life and take things as they came. And Tove gave Moomintroll

## Background, Ideas, and Influences

difficulties instead of adventures" (24). It was this same Tuulikki Pietilä who served as the model for Tooticki in <u>Moominland Midwinter</u> and <u>The Invisible Child</u>, the mentor who induces Moomintroll to accept the new reality with which he is surrounded.

The Moomintroll series continued until 1970, when the last of the novels, <u>Moominvalley in November</u>, appeared. Since then Moomin books have been sporadic and of a rather different nature--colored picture books with short texts. If, as appears to be the case, Tove Jansson has left the Moomins as her major work, it seems she is still tempted to take short, unassuming, and undemanding trips back into the fantasy world she created, a sign, perhaps, that although she has had to break new ground, the attraction of the children's books still remains. Again, she has commented on this:

> My first books were very naive and ordinary stories intended for very little children, but I feel that since then there has been a clear line . . . in my work, in the course of which my books have become less and less childish. I finally reached the point when I simply couldn't write for children any more. I think this is quite a natural change; perhaps I wasn't sufficiently childish myself any longer. (25)

And she goes on to say that her move from the Moomin books was regretted by many people, but that it was necessary.

> I am convinced that if a writer sits down with the sole intention of writing a children's book, the result will be poor. Whatever you do, you must do it because you <u>want</u> to do it, because of a <u>need</u> to express yourself in this way, and if you do it for any other reason the result will be pretty meagre. (26)

The question of literary influences inevitably arises, and the answer might at first seem surprising. Tove Jansson has herself listed some of them in a brief presentation of herself that she wrote in 1960:

> As a little girl I was very fond of Arosenius' <u>The Cat's Journey</u>, and then came Elsa Beskow and

Topelius (27). The books which made the greatest
impression on me as a young teenager were Kipling's
Jungle Book, Conrad's Typhoon, Poe's Tales of
Mystery and Imagination, Burroughs' first Tarzan
book, Curwood's Nomads of the North, Lagerlöf's
(28) Herr Arnes penningar (Sir Arne's Money),
Čapek's Krakatit, Hugo's Les travailleurs de la
mer, London's The Sea Wolf, Hardy's Far from the
Madding Crowd and Karlfeldt's (29) Vildmarksdikter (Poems of the heath).

In her interview with Bo Carpelan, she produces much
the same list, though she expands it slightly in a way
that throws a good deal of light on her own approach to
literature:

If everything goes wrong one day I can still take
out some of the romantic and naive fairy tales by
Topelius. Unless I choose science fiction or horror
stories. They calm me down. Take Ray Bradbury, for
instance: he works with such small means, but he
makes events credible. And so he has a calming
effect. (30)

She then adds that from the age of thirteen she avid-
ly read everything that came her way:

Ham--my mother--used to get the books for which she
designed covers, and I read everything she brought
home. If it was a book she thought unsuitable for
me--and she seldom thought that--all she needed to
do was say: this is a very worthwhile historical
novel, you should read it--and it remained unread.
When I was forced out to have some fresh air I sat
down behind a dustbin on the farm and went on reading. And at nights with an electric torch under the
bedclothes. (31)

In a letter, Tove Jansson has added Collodi's Pinocchio and Jules Verne's Captain Grant's Children to
these sources of inspiration, seeing the influence of
Pinocchio in Tulippa's blue hair in Comet in Moominland and of the Jules Verne novel in the idea of the
marooned Pappa sending his plea for help in a bottle
(32). On the other hand, she rejects what might look
like an obvious influence, A. A. Milne's Winnie the

Pooh, acknowledging certain similarities but stating that she did not read Milne until after she had started her own Moomin books.

Over the years Tove Jansson has become one of the most widely read of all Scandinavian authors. At the same time, she has had many exhibitions of her visual art and has been awarded a large number of prizes and medals, mainly for her books for children. Her fame as the creator of the Moomintrolls has spread still further, thanks to a number of television plays and series based on the Moomin family. She has also written a number of television plays for adults: "a little strange, with a touch of the horrific, to frighten the viewers" (33). She has written a number of radio plays of a similar nature.

Despite, or perhaps because of, the success of the series, the Moomin books have made great demands on her time and her imagination. Her increasing preoccupation with human psychology (often the abnormal or overdimensioned aspects of human personality, which was apparent in some of the later Moomin books and occasionally in the very early ones) meant that these books, originally conceived for children, became more and more disguised adult literature. Consequently, over the past ten years or so, Tove Jansson has experimented with various forms of adult literature--the semiautobiographical novel, the short story, the novel--and with works for radio and television. As she has become more at home in the adult genre, she has shown an increasing intensity, until her latest volume of short stories, The Doll's House, stands as a new climax to her work. Everything seems to indicate that she has now found a medium in which she can express herself more freely than she could in the Moomin books. With hindsight it is apparent that her work as a whole shows a clear line of development: the children's books gradually take on a new character and merge into adult literature. This development is the theme of the present study.

## Chapter Two
# The Little Trolls and the Great Flood

In 1945 a short and modest story for children appeared in Helsinki. It was called <u>The Little Trolls and the Great Flood</u>, written and illustrated by Tove Jansson. It was rather more than a run-of-the-mill children's book, certainly not a bad one, and the illustrations were competently done, even if they were in two distinct styles.

### The Action

Mamma and Moomintroll are seen in "the deepest valley" in the forest one afternoon toward the end of August. In true picaresque style, they are on a journey, the object of which does not clearly emerge at this stage. As they go into the forest, the light goes dim, and Moomintroll becomes afraid, whispering to his mother and asking whether there could be dangerous animals about. Mamma does not think so, but she decides that it might nevertheless be best to hurry. Even in this novel, she emerges as the symbol of security for her child and, subsequently, for the "little animal" whom they find on the way and who momentarily frightens her.

The journey is said to be a search for "a sunny spot to build a house" [5]. The Moomin habit of hibernating is referred to, and Mamma's instinctive desire to protect her family is plainly seen. The "little animal" joins them and is absorbed into the group, naturally and without further consideration. He is nervous, warns the others of dangers ahead, and insists that they are proceeding at their own risk--though having said this he joins in the expedition. Danger does approach in the evening darkness in the form of a serpent which is encountered after the light from a tulip has been extinguished. But suddenly a new light appears in the shape of a shining maiden who emerges from the tulip and lights up the scene with her blue hair. She is called Tulippa, and she, too, joins the little group.

14

# The Little Trolls and the Great Flood          15

The following morning, Tulippa serves a useful purpose when a spark from her hair is enough to light some tinder and start a fire round which the four can warm themselves, while Mamma tells of her younger days and explains that Moomintrolls used to live in stoves. She also tells of Pappa, who was always on the move until he finally went off with the strange hattifatteners, "the tiny wanderers." The suspicion that the journey might be intended to find him arises at this point, though it has not been obvious to now.

Mamma's weeping at the thought of her lost husband brings an old man to his door at the top of a tree. He invites the party inside to what at first appears to be a world of sunlight. However, it turns out to be an artificial world constructed by the old man, though the children approve of it as it is made of sugar and sweets and lemonade. Moomintroll and the little animal overeat before they all leave and go off on their search for the real sun. The suggestion that the ultimate object of their journey is to find Pappa is implicit but not stated overtly.

Once outside the artificial world, they find the "ocean," in which Moomintroll immediately starts bathing, accompanied by the little animal, while Tulippa, who is obviously made of more tender stuff, merely touches the water with her toes and finds it very cold. An ant lion is upset at being disturbed on the beach and almost buries Mamma in the sand, but the others save her at the last minute, after which they see a group of hattifatteners about to sail away. As Pappa has gone off with the hattifatteners, the various strands of the story appear now to merge. The party joins the hattifatteners, a storm comes on from which they are saved by sea trolls, and they all land on an unknown shore, a traditional desert island with palm trees, cacti, yams, and figs. They come across a strange house of gold in which they find a boy awaiting them. He has a meal of "sea pudding" for them, and when they then decide to resume their quest, Tulippa says she will stay behind; the blue-haired girl and the red-haired boy are obviously intended for each other.

The rain starts and continues through the night. In the morning, however, Mamma decrees that they must continue the search, even though the rain has caused serious flooding. After a long time the rain stops, and the sun appears. So does a bottle containing a message—from an unhappy moomintroll asking for help in his distress:

> Dear finder, Do what you can to save me! My house has been washed away by the floods, and now I am sitting lonely and hungry and cold in a tree as the water rises higher and higher. An unhappy moomintroll. [38]

As the waters recede, the family meets a somewhat testy hemulen. The little animal warns Mamma not to anger a hemulen, as he might bite—a characteristic that appears in the next novel but then disappears, to be replaced by the suggestion that hemulens on the whole are good-natured as long as they are not angered. The party also meets a maribu stork who has lost his spectacles. Moomintroll finds them, and in return the maribu takes him on his back to look for Pappa; later Mamma and the little animal go with them, with the obvious result that they finally find and rescue him.

As the waters recede yet further, they find Pappa's house, built rather like a stove, the traditional dwelling of the moomintrolls, standing in a beautiful fertile valley. It has been deposited by the floods in the place that is to become the home of the family throughout the rest of the Moomin stories: "And there in the valley they lived for the rest of their lives, apart from a couple of occasions when they went on journeys for the sake of a change" [48].

**Themes and Motifs**

The novel contains many motifs that recur in the later Moomin books. "The little animal," who meets up with Moomintroll and Mamma at the very beginning, stays with them and in the next novel becomes known as Sniff. He is the timid but selfish creature who constantly looks after his own interests. His cry that whatever they are doing must be on their own responsibility is repeated throughout the following book <u>Kometjakten</u> (<u>Comet in Moominland</u>) and is implicit in many of his actions in the later novels. He is, however, not yet fully developed, and the possibilities inherent in such a comic figure are by no means fully exploited.

Mamma is already in this short novel the kind mother who sees to the needs and comfort of all around her.

She is in authority, but her authority is gentle. Moomintroll accepts it, and even when he wants to go off on his own, he defers to his mother's wishes. In this particular episode, there is an early indication of Moomintroll's will to be independent, which later becomes a central feature of his makeup. Whether it is intended to be such is, of course, open to question, but it can certainly be read in this way. In view of the number of incidents and allusions that are taken up in Tove Jansson's later work, it is scarcely unnatural to see it as a forerunner of later events: "All day long they walked through the flowering countryside which the Moomintroll would have liked to investigate for himself. But his Mamma was in a hurry and wouldn't let him stay behind" [31].

Pappa is already the restless member of the family. His role throughout carries the threat of a potential breakup. His connection with the wandering hattifatteners is a constantly recurring theme in the later books, and on one occasion there is indeed an account of his "dissolute life" with them. However, there is no real indication here of any dissoluteness in his dealings with the hattifatteners, who are called only "foolish" and are portrayed as a group of constantly roving creatures without feelings. In later books, they become more sinister and appear to represent some layer of the subconscious in Pappa's personality--though the only time they actually cause a disturbance is when they and a hemulen are at cross purposes.

In one important respect, however, this story differs from the later ones, even from <u>Comet in Moominland</u>. It is much closer to the fairy tale than the others are, and it contains a magical element that is generally absent from Tove Jansson's work. The ending of <u>The Little Trolls and the Great Flood</u>, with its "happy ever after," is very much in tune with the popular fairy tale, but the magical element is seen more clearly at the beginning, first in the light from the tulip which the family uses to find its way through the forest, and then in the appearance of Tulippa, the tiny girl who lives in the tulip and whose hair radiates light which frightens away the serpent. Here is the flower fairy, reminiscent of Hans Christian Andersen's Thumbelina, and the episode must surely be seen as the good fairy conquering the evil serpent. That the fairy should find her prince is also part of the fairy tale, and that Tulippa does. Neither she nor the boy is referred to as a prince or princess, but the similarity is clear.

There is an element of danger in the adventures recounted in this first novel, though once more the pattern is somewhat different from that which was to emerge and assert itself in the later work. The pattern was to be that of the family, living in idyllic surroundings in Moomin Valley, being disturbed in some way, either by danger from outside or by some kind of internal crisis, and being forced to go through a series of adventures before returning to their accustomed peace and tranquility. Here the Moomintrolls do not at first appear to have a home, and Mamma is simply looking for a place in which to spend the winter. The "adventure" thus begins in a way not subsequently repeated, and it is scarcely even properly motivated, as the search for Pappa develops only part way through the story more or less as a coincidence. It is probably because of this basic difference in concept rather than anything else that Tove Jansson has never republished or reworked the story, as she was to do with Comet in Moominland. There, the basic theme of departure and return was established, but in The Little Trolls and the Great Flood, we are simply presented with a search--though it undoubtedly ends with the discovery of the Moomin Valley home which is essential to all the other books.

This, then, is a story that contains potential, a series of pre-echoes, rather than one that immediately places Tove Jansson in the forefront of children's writers. There are themes that were later to be worked out, and there are hints of relationships among members of the family and the creatures outside it that were also to be developed, and that, perhaps, as they became more and more complex helped to lead to the ultimate abandonment of the Moomintroll idea.

## Chapter Three
## *Comet in Moominland* and *The Comet Is Coming*

The second of Tove Jansson's Moomintroll novels, Kometjakten (Comet in Moominland), was published in 1946. A revised version then appeared in 1968 under the title of Kometen kommer (The comet is coming). It is the first version that formed the basis of the English translation, Comet in Moominland.

The 1968 version, which is shorter than that of 1946, represents a stylistic change and a tightening of the novel's structure rather than a radical alteration. It is psychologically more convincing, and numerous changes in metaphors indicate the author's increasing awareness of the importance of using the most appropriate metaphor for the occasion. Descriptive passages tend to be shorter and in many cases more apt (1), and the humor is at times more subtle and more appropriate, possibly slightly more "adult" than that in Comet in Moominland.

### The Plot in Two Versions

Like The Little Trolls and the Great Flood, Comet in Moominland is a book for children, as betokened by a number of parenthetical explanations and comments intended to guide the young reader's thoughts in the right direction. A picaresque novel with a happy ending, it serves to bring together a number of the characters who were later to play central roles in the Moomin stories. However, apart from being established in certain stock parts, they show little development, and they are scarcely interesting as characters in their own right. Once their particular, typical natures have been established, their reactions are consistently what can be expected of them.

From the start, the central characters are Moomintroll himself and Sniff. They go off together along a path that Sniff has found, meet a silk monkey, and end up by the sea. As in The Little Trolls and the Great Flood, Moomintroll goes for a swim and dives to the

19

bottom, while Sniff stays safe and dry. Together with
the monkey, Sniff goes along the cliffs where he finds
a cave. They discover a strange sign, a picture of a
star with a tail, which is repeated in various natural
phenomena. That night the muskrat appears in the
Moomin house. He is something of a philosopher (an
illustration shows him going to sleep over Spengler!),
and he interprets the mysterious sign as an indication
that a comet is approaching. Moomintroll and Sniff are
sent off to the observatory in the Lonely Mountains to
find out whether this is true and, if so, when the
comet will strike the earth. They sail away on a raft,
are attacked by a crocodile (an episode omitted in the
second version) and come up with a lonely person called
Snufkin. He joins them in their expedition: he is
solitary, calm and patient, a creature to whom peace of
mind is far more important than tangible possessions—
whereby he immediately forms a contrast to the self-
assertive and greedy Sniff. Because of his greed,
Sniff almost falls prey to a giant lizard, but he
manages to escape. After being swept into an underground stream and almost being washed into a bottomless
chasm, the three are rescued by a hemulen whose sole
interest is to collect as many butterflies as possible.
Like other hemulens in Tove Jansson's work, this one
is a collector, blinkered and unimaginative, within
limits good-tempered if not directly well-intentioned.

The three travelers leave the hemulen to his butterflies and proceed in search of the observatory, meeting
in true picaresque tradition with various brief
adventures on the way. Moomintroll finds a golden
bracelet which he assumes must have belonged to a Snork
Maiden whom Snufkin told him about and who fired his
imagination. On arriving at the observatory, Moomintroll is more interested in discovering whether the
Snork Maiden has been there than he is in the comet
that they came to enquire about. It is left to Sniff
to discover the exact time at which the comet is
expected to strike the earth, whereafter they decide to
make for the safety of Moomin Valley as quickly as
possible, though Moomintroll is keen to save the Snork
Maiden in the process.

On the way they meet with the hemulen again, and
then they hear cries for help issuing from the Snork
Maiden who has been caught by a poisonous man-eating
bush. Moomintroll takes out his knife and, like a true

knight errant, rescues the damsel from a terrible death. She and her brother, the Snork, now join the party.

The comet is steadily coming closer and closer, affecting the color of the sky and drying everything up. When the travelers reach the seashore there is no sea, and at the suggestion of Snufkin, they fit themselves out with stilts in order to walk across the ocean bed. They find a treasure chest, and Sniff manages to acquire a golden dagger--but in so doing he causes the Snork Maiden to fall into a sunken ship, where the brave and noble Moomintroll goes to rescue her, very nearly to fall prey to an octopus lurking in the darkness. Finally they arrive home to find Mamma and Pappa waiting for them. They have little time left, but they remove their belongings to Sniff's cave and there await the moment of impact. In fact, the comet narrowly misses the earth and recedes. The danger is past, and the novel ends with a picture of nature once more assuming its usual shape.

In the revised version, certain changes are made in this plot. The silk monkey is replaced by a kitten with which the egotistic Sniff tries to get on good terms; one of his few positive actions is to go out into the woods to find and save the kitten immediately before the comet is expected to strike the valley. The result is that Moomintroll has to go and save <u>him</u>! The first version is simpler: the silk monkey is lost, and Moomintroll goes out to find him. Another change effected in the second version is the removal of the crocodile scene--although the fantastic element is retained, greater attention is paid to a kind of verisimilitude, and there are simply no crocodiles in Finland! Yet another modification is the toning down of the wind that finally blows the party back to Moomin Valley and that in the first version was highly personified, even to the extent of having "windlets."

### The Characters Emerge

The characters are almost without exception stereotypes. Mamma is again the source of all security, always seen and portrayed with her handbag, and Pappa is a slightly more worried version of her. Sniff is self-centered, mercenary, greedy, and far more timid than he likes to admit. Moomintroll is more balanced, though he does give in to his romantic instincts in his infatuation with the Snork Maiden. She herself is pretty and empty-headed, and her brother is an eternal organizer with little sense of what is really important. The hemulen has even less sense of the important, obsessed as he is with his passion for collecting and interested only in not being disturbed. The indolent muskrat makes little contribution to his surroundings, whereas Snufkin, in contrast, is a philosopher of a different kind who loves the beauty of nature and has little interest in worldly goods. He is an artist, a musician who plays the mouth organ and who can either recapture or create atmosphere.

Moomintroll is the central figure in the novel, though this is perhaps more because of the obvious significance of the Moomin family than because of any innate qualities. He is a child filled with childish enthusiasm and a good deal of childish bravado, as when he dives to the bottom of the sea or when he reacts to the sober, unenthusiastic muskrat's remark about unnecessary journeys with: "But I love making journeys. . . . There are hardly any unnecessary things, I think. Only eating porridge and washing" (25) [40]. This comment, omitted in The Comet Is Coming, serves to underline Moomintroll's unreflected energy and perhaps also to foreshadow the journey into the Lonely Mountains. In general, however, Moomintroll is revealed more through his relations with the other characters than in his own right. Vis-à-vis Sniff he is even-tempered and determined; to Mamma he is the gentle child, the boy who longs to get back home; to Snufkin he is the small friend, and the burgeoning friendship between the two is clearly to be seen. Most obvious, however, is his infatuation with the Snork Maiden (perhaps a very early sign of the obsession theme which plays a central part in Tove Jansson's late work) and the consistent portrayal of him as a knight errant. In Comet in Moominland, he is even specifically described as being chivalrous in the way in which he speaks to the Snork Maiden, a comment that is, however, removed from the more down-to-earth account in The Comet Is Coming.

## The Different Versions

The second edition of the novel, The Comet Is Coming, is without doubt an improvement on the first, though the changes are not so radical that the two can be considered as separate works. Descriptions are more realistic and more closely related to the action. Individual reactions in specific situations are changed so as to make them more acceptable. Comments and discussions are altered and made more credible. The intention is generally clearer, and superfluous episodes and characters are removed. The transitions from one episode to another are made neater. Fantasy there still is, but it is kept more under control--so the Snork Maiden's propensity for changing color according to mood is toned down in the second version. By 1968, when it was published, Tove Jansson was a far more practiced writer than she had been in 1946. She has moreover modernized her text, removing certain features that would obviously date it, either by the simple updating of prices or else by the removal of dateable terms: whereas in Comet in Moominland the Snork Maiden asks Moomintroll whether he can dance "swing"--thus placing it firmly in its decade--the question in The Comet Is Coming is: "Can you dance these new things, whatever you call them?" [113]. That question is timeless. However, the drawing illustrating the scene is unchanged, and it is obvious from it that Moomintroll and the Snork Maiden are at any rate dancing differently from anyone else.

While there is an ironical element in the portrayal of Moomintroll's infatuation with the vain and empty-headed Snork Maiden, this novel shows the start of a more significant friendship with Snufkin. Although relatively little is seen of him, he is the Bohemian who stands outside convention, a figure who later comes to play an important part in fashioning Moomintroll, perhaps at times appearing as the author's own mouthpiece. He is the artist, with the artist's sensitivity and the artist's particular kind of self-sufficiency. When he has pointed to the beauty of the landscape, both Moomintroll and Sniff realize there is something special about him:

> "You aren't by any chance--er--a painter?" asked Moomintroll rather shyly.
> "Or perhaps a poet?" suggested Sniff.
> "I am everything!" said Snufkin, putting on the kettle. (54) [47]

Almost symbolically, his tent is the first patch of

color Moomintroll and Sniff have seen on their journey downstream; his welcome is warm and yet reflects the calm with which he approaches any situation. When they are being swept along by the underground stream and he senses danger, it is he who quickly understands the situation and gives the right orders--with sufficient quiet authority to be sure of being obeyed.

Only once does Snufkin lose his calm exterior, and that is when they discover that the sea has dried up. Here the two versions are different, though Snufkin's worries are the same. In <u>Comet in Moominland</u> Moomintroll has to comfort him: "But Snuff," said Moomintroll reproachfully, "you have always been so happy-go-lucky. It's dreadful to see you despairing like this" (110) [123]. There is less obvious despair portrayed in <u>The Comet Is Coming</u>:

> Moomintroll sat down beside him and said, "It'll be all right. Everything'll be all right when the comet has gone. Don't you think so?"
> But Snufkin made no reply. [100-101]

And with this Moomintroll knows that things are really bad.

It is quite obvious in this scene that there is a special link between Moomintroll and Snufkin, and this link is strengthened and developed throughout the remainder of the series. It is more clearly emphasized in <u>The Comet Is Coming</u> than in <u>Comet in Moominland</u>, and it is worth remembering that <u>The Comet Is Coming</u> was written after the author had fully developed the Moomintroll-Snufkin relationship in the novels written in the intervening years.

Meanwhile, it emerges quite clearly that even in 1946 Tove Jansson had some idea of what was to come later: there are references to Pappa's writing his memoirs, which were not published until later, and there are further allusions to his "dissolute" life with the hattifatteners. Nevertheless, subsequent developments could scarcely have been clear when the first version was written, and so it was necessary in this respect, too, to update it and make the second version fit the series better than the first now did. Even the illustrations in the second edition are slightly modified, Moomintroll and his parents being rounder and more like the "finished" Moomintrolls in the later work. From the point of view of the illustrator's technique, the first two volumes in the series distinguish themselves from the rest. They were a beginning, and they needed modifying. The revised version shows the result, and consequently <u>The Comet Is Coming</u> is dovetailed into the rest of the series.

## Chapter Four
## *Finn Family Moomintroll*

<u>Finn Family Moomintroll</u> was the first of the Moomin books to be published in English (in 1950), which presumably explains why a title was chosen that is so far from the original and that in fact bears singularly little relationship to the contents. The Swedish title, <u>Trollkarlens hatt</u>, means "the magician's hat."

However, despite its title, the novel is not about a magician's hat, either (1). Nor, for that matter, is it really about a magician, though both play a part in it. To some extent the magician's hat acts as a catalyst, but it has nothing to do with the Moomin family's trip to the hattifattener island, which in one sense lies at the center of the action; nor does it play any part in the last chapter, by which time it has been taken by the Groke as she leaves Moomin Valley. On the other hand, the magician himself is glimpsed by Snufkin while they are all on the hattifattener island, and in the last chapter he finally puts in a real appearance to the accompaniment of a good deal of melodrama and behaves as a more or less traditional good fairy.

### Another Picaresque Novel

In fact, after a short prelude showing the Moomin family preparing to hibernate, the entire book is concerned with events of the next spring and summer after they have awakened again. In their delight at the return of spring, Moomintroll and Sniff go out into the mountains and there find what turns out to be the magician's hat. They take it home, after which ensues the series of events around which parts of the story are built. The obvious use for the hat is as a wastepaper basket, and thus some eggshells are thrown into it. They turn into small clouds with which the children can play and on which they can even ride. (Clouds of a not entirely dissimilar nature are met again in <u>The Exploits of Moominpappa</u>.) Moomintroll himself hides in the hat and emerges to find his shape changed, after which he realizes what is going on and puts the hat to his own purposes to transform an ant lion. Mamma also understands the situation and wisely decides to get rid of the hat, but she only throws it into the river, which it promptly turns into a river of fruit juice. Snufkin and Moomintroll retrieve it, putting it into a cave where it is found by the muskrat, who deposits his false teeth in it with dire consequences. Exactly what those consequences are is never stated, but it is obviously a terrifying experience for the rat.

This episode takes place as the family is on its way to a desert island. They find a boat and sail off, and on arriving at their destination, they once more meet the hattifatteners, now more clearly described as strange electric people who have no sense of sound and little eyesight. The magician is glimpsed as he flies by. A great storm ensues, and the hemulen, tactless as ever, has a frightening confrontation with the hattifatteners, but all comes well in the end, and the family return home with all the exciting things they have found on the island. The magician's hat now goes into action again when Mamma throws into it a plant found by the hemulen: it turns into a jungle filling the whole house, and is enjoyed by everyone except the poor, uncomprehending hemulen.

Two strange creatures called Thingumy and Bob then arrive, bringing with them the King's Ruby; they are soon followed by the Groke, a strange cold creature who finally makes off with the magician's hat. In the final chapter, the magician himself, who has spent his life searching for the King's Ruby, sees it in Moomin Valley in the bag carried by Thingumy and Bob, and comes to take possession of it. He fails to persuade them to give it to him as they have received it from the Groke in exchange for the magician's hat, but despite his disappointment, the magician promises to grant everyone a wish. When it comes to the turn of Thingumy and Bob, they wish for a Queen's Ruby identical to the King's Ruby, and this they give to the magician. The book then finishes with the celebrations in honor of this event.

There are once more obvious elements of the fairy tale in <u>Finn Family Moomintroll</u>, and there are certain similarities to the picaresque novel, if the progress from spring to late summer rather than merely a physical journey is taken as the basis. And, as often happens in a picaresque novel, there are the elements of a search, perhaps of several searches that finally merge: there is the magician's search for the Ruby, coupled with the Groke's desire to possess it, while in the background there is a comical parallel--pointed out by Snufkin--in the hemulen's obsessive mania for collecting. The question obviously is whether any particular significance should be attached to the Ruby or to the gifts dispensed by the magician at the end. Snufkin's account in chapter 5 of how the magician collects rubies seems to indicate that this is the case.

**A Moral?**

If the parallel be drawn with the hemulen's craze for collecting, then the acquisition of the King's Ruby will only cause dissatisfaction and frustration in the magician, but Snufkin's suggestion that he will not be happy until he has found it does perhaps imply that he will be happy once he has achieved his objective. And indeed, on finding the Ruby, the magician, who has so far been presented as a vaguely menacing figure, soon melts and adopts a kindly attitude. He even accepts that he cannot own it. But in one sense, he has achieved his purpose by simply finding it.

An interpretation of the significance of the Ruby must of necessity be imprecise, but if the positive results of the magician's quest are seen in contrast to the hemulen's desire to collect and also to Sniff's acquisitiveness, the book becomes a novel about the interplay of acquisitiveness and the creation of happiness, of selfishness as opposed to benevolence. Whatever his pleasure in collecting, the hemulen achieves no happiness through it, and neither does Sniff gain anything from his determined efforts to feather his own nest. But the magician creates happiness, and so does Mamma. So, in his way, does Snufkin, who in fact desires nothing but is happy with it:

> . . . Snufkin could never understand why people liked to <u>have</u> things. He was quite happy wearing the old suit he had had since he was born . . . and the only possession he didn't give away was his mouth organ. (21) [17-18]

### Snufkin and Moomintroll

Through the person of Snufkin, the idea of being satisfied with what life sends is established as central to the story, and it is implied in the happy song he plays on his mouth organ: "All small beasts should have bows in their tails"; the same song is heard at the end of the book as he disappears from sight on his winter travels. (It emerges elsewhere in the novels and takes on something of the character of a leitmotiv.) Snufkin is different from all the other characters in this book, though he has that inner harmony that is also found in Mamma. The special relationship between him and Moomintroll is indicated from the very first, when Moomintroll wants to hibernate in the same room. When he wakes up to discover that Snufkin has gone, he immediately goes out to look for him.

At this, the first detailed account of the closeness that has developed between them, the ideals of the work are expressed both directly and indirectly: indirectly through the picture of the two of them unconcernedly sitting swinging their legs over the stream while the sun shines on them, and directly by the comment that they both feel "happy and carefree." Just as Snufkin is here able to derive a direct and simple enjoyment of life from his surroundings and as he does on the shore of the island, so, too, he does when the whole family goes bathing: "Snufkin was floating on his back far out and looking up into the blue and gold sky" (78) [76]. Apart from this, he is shown to love solitude and to possess imagination, tact, and a good deal of humor: when the blustering hemulen complains that he is in difficulties with the hattifatteners and asks why an innocent botanist cannot be allowed to live in peace and quiet, Snufkin comments that life is not a peaceful affair; he omits to add that the hemulen has been anything but an innocent botanist, and that he has brought on himself the trouble he is in.

The close friendship between Moomintroll and Snufkin develops quickly in these books and seems to reflect something of the intimacy and understanding that can arise between a child and a grown-up who is simply an experienced, wise friend without a relative's built-in authority. The closeness is seen not only in Moomintroll's actual decision to go and find Snufkin but in the fact that he can sense Snufkin's mood from his footprints on the wet ground. An even clearer statement comes later: "What about it?" asked Snufkin's eyebrows, and Moomintroll's ears waggled a big "Yes" (44) [41]. It is with Snufkin that Moomintroll for the first time does something he cannot tell his parents about; it is beside the point that the action he undertakes is an innocent one--an attempt to avoid complications by retrieving the magician's hat from the river and putting it in a safe place. In the course of the novels, Moomintroll undergoes a profound transformation; it is possible to see an episode like this as showing the child's dawning independence of action, something not found in the first of the novels when he does as his mother wishes.

Throughout this book, Moomintroll is a gentle, kind creature, a child who has many of the positive features of his mother and father and who is attracted by a Snufkin with those same qualities minus the parental authority. He is upset when the others mock him for his appearance when he has been transformed, but when he realizes that the hat must be capable of magic, he refuses to take his revenge by enticing anyone else into it, in case that are irreversibly transformed. He is still fond of the Snork Maiden, though his obsession has perhaps developed into a calmer form of devotion, and he uses quite poetical language to her and of her. He shares Snufkin's appreciation of nature, as is clearly revealed during their visit to the island: he has a sense of wonderment which is lacking in all the other little ones, by which he is immediately placed apart from them. His potential is not yet clear in Finn Family Moomintroll, although the greater depth of his personality is obvious, and this is underlined by his profound but unspoken sadness on learning that Snufkin has gone for the winter.

**Mamma and Pappa**

Typically, it is Mamma who realizes what is wrong with him, and it is typical, too, that her wish to the magician is that the sorrow should be taken away from him. This, if nothing else, would indicate what Mamma stands for in this novel. She is more securely than ever the central figure in the family. She exudes warmth, peace, and contentment, and she is directly identified with the home and all that it represents.

*Finn Family Moomintroll*

In the preparations for hibernation with which the book begins, it is Mamma who is, gently, in charge. And when, the following spring, Moomintroll and Snufkin and Sniff are out in the mountains and catch a glimpse of the house from afar, Mamma is identified with its homeliness: ". . . to the south the smoke rose from Moomintroll's chimney, for Moominmamma was cooking the breakfast" (18) [14]. This is the epitome of home comfort. The house is always open to all the new friends who are brought to it: "Moomintroll's mother and father always welcomed all their friends in the same quiet way, just adding another bed and putting another leaf in the dining-room table" (15-16) [12]. When Thingumy and Bob arrive, this is immediately confirmed, and it is Mamma who sums up the situation:

> Then she caught sight of the suitcase which stood by the steps. "Luggage, too," thought Moominmamma. "Dear me--then they've come to stay." And she went off to look for Moominpappa to ask him to put up two more beds--very very small ones. (115) [113]

Not only is she aware of the need to make up fresh beds, but her sense of comfort tells her that they must be small. Her instinctive need to understand what other people want is further underlined in the same episode, when she realizes that she does not understand the language spoken by the two newcomers: "How shall I be able to find out what they want for pudding on their birthday, or how many pillows they like to have?" (116) [114].

Her sense of comfort and care means that it is she who discovers the right name for the boat they find when going to their island: the rather pretty-pretty Snork Maiden has her The Pee-wit scorned, while her determined brother's Sea Eagle is refused by the hemulen. His own pedantic and unimaginative Moominates Maritima is ignored by Sniff, who with his customary love of himself wants to call it Sniff. Even Snufkin's poetic Lurking Wolf finds no approval, and it is Mamma's straightforward and homely The Adventure that is finally accepted by all. This charming and amusing scene, in which the character of each person concerned is reflected in the names suggested, ends with a vindication of Mamma's uncomplicated understanding of what is desirable.

On arriving on the island, Mamma is again the one who sees to everyone else's needs: it is she who collects stones to build a fireplace on which to warm the food they have brought with them, she who buries the butter in order to keep it from the heat, and she who refuses a rather belated offer of help from Moomintroll:

"You can explore the island," said Moominmamma (who knew that was what they were longing to do). "It's important to know where we've landed. It could be dangerous, couldn't it?" (61) [58]

Her concern in case of danger is typical of her and echoes her words on seeing Moomintroll on his little "cloud" in the beginning, when she expresses neither surprise nor consternation, but only the hope that he will be careful not to fall off. Nothing seems to surprise her. Her inner harmony is so strong that one of the first things she does on landing on the island is to gather flowers to decorate their primitive table. And after the day's adventures and the terrible storm, it is Mamma who tucks in everyone else and, significantly, goes to sleep with her handbag under her pillow. Such is her inner peace that she sleeps, apparently, throughout the invasion by the hattifatteners, and after the chaos caused by the hemulen when he brings down the tent, she emerges, still with her bag in her hand, to suggest that they should perhaps try to put it up again and get some more sleep. When in the morning the Snork Maiden discovers that the hattifatteners have burned off her hair, Mamma is the one to find the right means of consolation by telling the vain creature that not only will her hair grow again but that it will be curly. (In contrast, the hemulen comforts the girl by telling her that _he_ has always quite liked being bald!)

There can be no doubt as to the harmony existing between Mamma and Pappa, but Pappa's role is less essential than Mamma's. She leads; he merely complies, though at times she gives in to what she knows to be his wishes: when it is decided that they should go for a sail and try to find an island, it is Mamma who organizes things, though she remarks that Pappa wants to get off straight away. His subsequent actions tend to confirm this, and they also show him to be fond of organizing. When, for once, things go slightly wrong and Mamma forgets the fruit juice, he shows himself to be capable of slight irritation. However, he is peaceful enough, and his main preoccupations are, perhaps, fishing, to which there are various references, and making things for the family. When they are all looking for what has been washed up on the shore, he finds wood to build a jetty--and he does indeed build it. However, he wants to do this and everything else on his own and refuses help from Snufkin. There is a certain pompous independence about Pappa, which emerges on more than one occasion.

One feature of Pappa's actions in the novel is a slight indication that he is, or feels himself to be, in contact with the sea. He considers the boat they find to be a gift from the sea, and he looks optimistically to the same source later when the storm has swept over the island and Mamma's butter has disappeared. He brushes aside her concern about what to give the family on their bread:

> "Never mind," said Moominpappa. "We'll see if the storm has given us something else instead. After coffee we'll make a tour of inspection along the beach and see what the sea has washed up!" And this they did. (79) [76]

The quotation again suggests that the sea is expected to <u>give</u> something. This could, of course be a mere figure of speech, but if these brief remarks are compared with what happens in the later novel, <u>Moominpappa at Sea</u>, it does appear as though Pappa, perhaps more than the facts justify, feels that he has some secret link or affinity with the sea. At the same time, it should be noted that the sea is clearly personified in the description of its behavior during the storm.

### Other Characters

To say that Snufkin, Moomintroll, Mamma, and Pappa are the positive characters in this novel, as opposed to a group of negative figures, would be an exaggeration. Only one "person" is entirely negative, the Groke (and even she thaws out in the later work). Sniff and the hemulen are figures of fun at the same time as they represent two types not entirely unknown in the world of human beings.

Sniff is as self-centered as ever. Mention has already been made of his suggestion of a name for the boat, and this is, of course, symptomatic. His attitude is apparent from the start, for when he and Moomintroll and Snufkin go to the top of the mountain and find the hat, he is the one to express disappointment because someone has obviously been on the mountain peak before them. He has already shown his bad temper at being awakened early--he has the habit of sleeping for a week longer than the rest--and he shows his desire to dominate the others by appointing himself referee in the game on the clouds, which means that he sails slightly higher than anyone else. It also means that he does not expose himself to the danger of being knocked off. His nervousness is once more a characteristic that is often noticed: he stays in the shallow water when the others go bathing, and when the family is sitting on the beach after the storm, he makes sure that he is in the middle of the row, for that is where he feels safest. As he is always careful to ensure his own comfort and safety (he dives under the table when he thinks he is being threatened by an ant lion), so he always looks to his own advantage, as when the muskrat rushes away and Sniff immediately sees the chance of eating the food he must have left behind. It goes almost without saying that when Pappa is showing signs of not knowing what to wish for himself from the magician, Sniff sees the possibility of having an extra wish instead. And when he does have his wish, it is a big one.

The other principal figure of fun is the hemulen. In some ways, he almost acts as a satirical counterpart to Mamma and Pappa, a "grown-up" who tends to stay with them rather than enjoy himself with the smaller members of the party. He is comical because he always wears a dress (as, we are told, do all hemulens), looking rather like a more angular and ungainly version of a Moomin, if one is to judge from the illustrations. He is fundamentally well-intentioned, but he is completely lacking in imagination; he is obsessive and noticeably slow on the uptake; he has no sense of beauty.

His slowness to observe things is seen early in the book when Moomintroll and Sniff approach him on their clouds. He speaks to them but does not notice what

they are standing on. This lack of perception has its
counterpart in many of the later episodes, where it may
well appear as a lack of intuition as, for instance,
when he is the only one who fails to go into the
jungle-filled house. While the others inside make the
most of their unusual situation, he sits outside the
door, faithfully keeping watch over the "mameluke" and
counting the number of stamens on a jungle flower,
oblivious to what is otherwise going on:

> All this time the Hemulen was rambling about in the
> wood, enraptured by the masses of rare flowers.
> They were not like the flowers that grew in Moomin
> Valley--oh, far from it! Heavy, silvery-white
> clusters which looked as if they were made of glass;
> crimson-black kingcups like royal crowns, and sky-
> blue roses.
> But the Hemulen didn't see much of their beauty--
> he was too busy counting the stamens and leaves, and
> muttering to himself: "This is the two hundred-and-
> nineteenth specimen in my collection!" (63) [60]

He has gone in for collecting flowers after deciding
that he now has a complete stamp collection, for which
reason it is no longer of interest. His obsession with
flowers is exemplified when he is quite early on seen
counting the stamens of a sunflower, and later, though
less explicitly, when he is found digging up a rare
orchid. He has no respect for flowers, no sense of
their beauty, merely the urge to acquire as many speci-
mens as possible. The lack of insight this covers over
often leaves him open to ridicule, for he never understands anything that is not spelled out in detail:
"Will someone please tell me what all this is about,"
he says (40) [37], when he is together with Moomintroll, Sniff, and the Snork Maiden and fails to understand what they are doing when they try to entice the
ant lion into the hat. Likewise, when the others
realize that it is the magician's hat that has been
causing all the trouble, the hemulen still fails to see
it: "'What's that,' enquired the hemulen. 'What are
you talking about?'" (94) [93]. His slowness can lead
him into trouble. Despite warnings not to irritate the
hattifatteners, he does so (though his remark about
being an innocent botanist indicates that perhaps he
does not realize what he has done). When they return

to find their barometer, he is the last to realize they are there, and is only awakened when one of them treads on his nose, after which he makes such a fuss that he brings down the tent. When it comes to his wish, it is a modest one, but entirely in keeping with his behavior: a botanist's spade. And as he makes his wish, this large, clumsy male curtsies.

**Humor and Poetry**

Finn Family Moomintroll is a book of adventures large and small, but it is also a humorous book. Indeed, the entire idea of having a magic hat which causes confusion every time anything is put into it is an excellent recipe for comedy. Direct comedy there is, too, most obviously perhaps when the hemulen almost gets a fishing rod in his eye in the classical comedy situation. Nevertheless, it is typical of the gentleness of the story that he only nearly gets it in his eye. Or there is the entire episode around the muskrat's decision to withdraw to the cave and meditate.

Both these episodes, together with others of a similar nature, will of course be understood by children. They represent both an event and a brand of humor that will appeal to young readers. However, not all the humor will be appreciated by them. There is, in muskrat's decision to withdraw to the desert, an obvious element of subtle adult humor, partly in the decision to withdraw at all (the rat is a philosopher) and partly in his contrasting order to the family to bring him his food twice daily. There appears here to be a veiled reference to the early Christian hermits who went to live in the desert. To apply this association to an event in a book of this kind betokens humor of a sort not likely to be understood by all and certainly not by all children. Otherwise the adult humor tends to be found in the odd remark rather than in episodes, for instance, in the Snork's ironical comment to the hemulen when the poor creature cannot get through the jungle: "'Then you can stay outside and guard the mameluke,' said the Snork. 'You can botanize on the house now, can't you'" (109) [106]. And, as has been seen above, this is exactly what he does. The irony of the situation will be as lost on a child as it is on the hemulen, but the alert grown-up will spot it.

With the humor goes a delightful fantasy: the idea

of unexpected magical happenings issuing from a hat gives almost unlimited reign to the imagination, and indeed one amazing event after another occurs. Perhaps the most fantastic is the "Tarzan" episode, which consists of one fantasy superimposed upon another: the jungle is fantastic enough, but to use a fantasy jungle to allow the entire family to have a realistic game of Tarzan, even down to Tarzan's language, is producing an impressive logic of the imagination. And the more comical then, of course, becomes the poor hemulen outside.

Yet there is also poetry in the novel. The descriptions of the sea, of the storm, of the nature on the island, have a beauty of their own, which is preparing the reader for the symbolical poetry in some of the later work. The sea is personified, and so is the island, in a way that will appeal to adults rather than to children.

To talk of any kind of analysis of human beings would still be out of place. Tove Jansson continues to operate on easily identified general characteristics. But precisely because of this, her characters are immediately acceptable to the less sophisticated reader, while the humor behind the portrayal makes them satisfying to those who demand more of a novel. For the adult, the poetry, the humor, the inventiveness, the linguistic skill of the writer supplement those aspects of the story that are of immediate appeal to children. It is this combination of qualities that is characteristic of the Moomin books, and it is the increasing emphasis placed on the adult elements in the later ones that brought Tove Jansson to the conclusion that she must move away from the children's book to a different form of reality.

*Chapter Five*
# The Exploits of Moominpappa

Despite its memoir-like character, this novel is again fundamentally in the picaresque style, though it has obvious affinities with other novel types, not least the Robinson Crusoe school. Moreover, it seeks to combine, not entirely successfully, the more or less realistic aspect of Tove Jansson's work with the fantastic. Of the eight chapters, the first four are "realistic," after which we move into an increasingly fantastic world. The "action" ends with a scene reminiscent of a stage show, with the various characters being gathered together in festive circumstances, while the actual book itself ends with a grand reunion some forty years after the events described.

As happens in many of the old works of memoirs by which these appear to be inspired, Pappa is hoping not only to portray himself and tell of his experiences, but also to pass on his wisdom to others. That there is also an element of self-aggrandizement in his memoirs might or might not be due to the genre that inspired them.

**Moominpappa by Moominpappa**

According to his account, Pappa was left in a paper bag outside an orphanage run by a female hemulen. She took him in and brought him up to be a well-behaved and well-disciplined child in circumstances and surroundings that were alien to him and his innermost nature. He disliked the home and ran away, leaving behind him the inevitable note to the hemulen. He now wanders off into a forest, and, out of his deepest instincts, builds himself a Moomin house, which is vaguely reminiscent of a stove, the very antithesis of the hemulen's orphanage. (Moomintrolls once lived in stoves in the distant past, it should be remembered.) The fugitive tries without success to make contact with his surroundings, until a creature with what in the Moomin context is the unlikely name of Hodgkins appears. The two decide to combine forces, and Moominpappa's house and the boat that Hodgkins is building are joined together to produce a houseboat. They are now joined by the Joxter, a vague and easygoing creature who turns out to be the father of Snufkin, and the Muddler, a self-centered little thing who is subsequently identified as Sniff's father. The houseboat is finished and (badly) painted, and it is launched when the enormous and somewhat unpredictable Edward the Booble is persuaded to sit in the river and dam it, thus providing sufficient depth of water. During the voyage upon which they now embark, Pappa saves a hemulen from being eaten by the Groke; she makes their life on board unbearable until she is carried off by a horde of niblings, tiny, sticky sea creatures who have the tendency to eat anything in sight, especially large noses--and hemulens have large noses. The party sails into a storm and is saved when three small clouds they succeed in capturing manage to tow them to safety.

At this stage, we move into the even more fantastic second half of the story, for now the party meets the Mymble's daughter, a child who has many of the characteristics of Little My, whom we meet in later books and who turns out to be her sister. The Mymble's daughter takes the friends to a festival arranged to celebrate the hundredth birthday of the local king, who calls himself Daddy Jones. A mixture of royalty and the ordinary rather like Hans Christian Andersen's Chinese Emperor, he is treated with great deference by the royalist Moominpappa. His festivities are characterized by a variety of practical jokes, and the prizes he gives to those who find the numbered eggs hidden around the park are carefully chosen to reflect the kind of intelligence attributable to a person likely to look in that particular spot. (A parallel is seen here to the fulfillment of the wishes granted by the magician in the earlier book.) Hodgkins is taken on by the king as his inventor, and the group now moves across to a small island and sets up a colony in which there are to be no laws. A ghost appears, but however much it tries to frighten them, it cannot. All it can do is join them, which it does: it even appears at the reunion at the end of the book. Hodgkins has now constructed his new "Amphibian," a mixture of airplane and submarine. After a short and uneventful flight, they dive beneath the waves, where they are almost destroyed by a "sea hound," but are saved at the last moment when Edward the Booble turns up and unwittingly crushes it with his foot. On returning to the mainland, they discover that the Muddler has married; the wedding celebration is the occasion that brings together all the characters, though the seven thousand niblings prefer to stay behind with the hemulen whom they carried off, as she constantly entertains them with guessing games. Finally comes the account of how Pappa met Mamma when, clutching her handbag, she was washed ashore by a gigantic wave. It was a case of love at first sight. The Epilogue is of no real significance to the story, though the arrival of his friends does perhaps seem to indicate that Pappa has been telling a story at least partly based on the truth, something that the reader at times might have been justified in doubting.

### The Real Pappa

Like any "autobiography," <u>The Exploits of Moominpappa</u> raises the question of reliability. As has already been apparent in <u>Finn Family Moomintroll</u>, Pappa is inclined to be boastful and somewhat pompous. These characteristics, which follow him throughout the Moomin series, inevitably color his own presentation of himself here, and thereby allow the <u>real</u> author to indulge in the mixture of tolerance and irony that have evinced themselves in the earlier book. Indeed, it allows her to go much further, for she has her view, and he has his, and the two become inextricably interwoven. Pappa admits in the introduction that he has embellished certain events, and the various versions he gives of the wrappings in which he was left on the hemulen's steps as a baby leave the reader in no doubt as to his ability to exaggerate. At the same time, if we are to judge from the short interludes in his account, he appears to avoid talking of his relationship with the hattifatteners, whose "wicked" dissolute life arouses the fascination of his listeners. The attraction that the ceaseless wanderings of the hattifatteners have for him is by now clearly established.

There is in fact no real indication anywhere in the series that Pappa ever seriously embarks on the dissolute life ascribed to the hattifatteners, though he does make contact with them. Indeed, we have only the Joxter's word for it that the hattifatteners do in fact lead a dissolute life. In a story such as this where he is both boasting and trying to make himself interesting if not important, it is obvious that Pappa will be tempted to hint at an "interesting" episode in his life that he is not prepared to divulge. Yet at the same time, the hattifatteners and his attitude toward them can be seen on a different level. They obviously appeal to his desire to travel, to the restless, escapist element in him, and equally obviously, they appeal to his baser instincts which are otherwise thoroughly suppressed, except on the occasion on which he disappears for a time in order to join them. At all events, his interest is quickly awakened when Hodgkins talks of their constant traveling, and when the Joxter speaks of their "wicked" life, his curiosity becomes intensified: "'A wicked life,' I repeated with interest. 'How?'" (52) [60]. The Joxter's reply is vague and innocent—or evasive: perhaps they trample on people's gardens, or they drink beer! This is scarcely the kind of thing to attract Pappa, even if he accepts the Joxter's reply at its face value. If Pappa is to be taken seriously, it appears that there is a hidden Bohemian element in him which is suppressed by his present bourgeois respectability:

> We sat there for a long time looking after the Hattifatteners sailing out towards the horizon. I really couldn't help it, but I felt a vague desire to join them on their voyage and to share their wicked life for a while. But I didn't say it. (52) [60]

It is this element, the need to realize himself after his oppressive childhood and his mildly bourgeois adult life, that finally moves him in Moominpappa at Sea to sail away with his family to his island, and the urge then seems to be satisfied, for in Moominvalley in November the indication is that the family returns to the security offered by Moomin Valley. One may again wonder whether Pappa is genuine in talking of the way in which he is attracted by the hattifatteners, but the fact that he subsequently does make contact with them indicates that here, at least, he is telling a form of the truth.

The possibility of a deep split in Pappa's nature and of suppressed but nonunderstood urges is shown at a much earlier stage in the book while he is still living

in the orphanage. He tries, unsuccessfully, to discuss
life with the hemulen, asking why he is what he is and
why he is not someone else. He cannot find the answer,
and at first the question seems aimed at throwing the
hemulen into relief, as she cannot even see the point
of it. Nor can she see the argument that the disobedi-
ent Moomintroll that Pappa has dreamed himself to be
might conceivably be the real one. Pappa himself does
not understand the significance of this, either, though
it seems likely to be an early example of suppressed
facets of Pappa's personality making themselves felt
through dreams. The immediate implication that the
hemulen has no imaginative power may in fact be too
superficial an interpretation of this entire scene.
The following episode seems to have a similar psychological implication: Pappa, as a child, stands on the
ice and looks through it into the hidden world beneath
the surface, a world that is alien to him but in fact
is as real as the one of which he is conscious:

> There I saw a world that was quite new to me, a
> green and dark world reaching further and further
> down. . . . The black fingers of seaweed were
> stretching out to touch the ice, and a strange
> creature on eight stiff legs was crawling about on
> the sand. He went off into the darkness of the
> ocean depths, all alone. I stared down, deeper and
> deeper, until I felt sick with fear. Then I looked
> up from the ice and saw nothing but the sky again,
> with gentle clouds scudding about. Can anyone
> imagine anything more remarkable?
> "Suppose I fell in," I thought. It was such a
> dreadful thought that I had to think it again: Deep-
> er and deeper . . . Never more! Just further and
> further down. (1)

This passage, with obvious Freudian overtones, again
seems to suggest not only a glimpse of the world
beneath the water but also a glimpse beneath the
surface of Pappa's conscious self, a view of the hidden
sides of his nature--and he is frightened by what he
sees at the same time as being fascinated by it. Whatever philosophical or psychological overtones there may
be, however, are abruptly dispersed when Pappa falls
into that very world--and ends up being locked in a
punishment room as a naughty boy. Tove Jansson is

*The Exploits of Moominpappa*

quite obviously here working on two levels of understanding and appreciation. At the same time, there is a delicious sense of ironical humor, for in observing and questioning, Pappa does show himself to be on a higher intellectual level than the hemulen, and yet he has to be brought back to earth and put in his place.

He believes, of course, throughout that he is a genius, although this is constantly treated with the irony it deserves. From the start he sees himself as something extraordinary:

> Geniuses are generally thought of as being rather unpleasant people, but I can't say this has ever worried me. (2)

There is no mistaking his judgment of himself here, and his confidence in his infallibility persists. The house he builds is something he obviously thinks of as a masterpiece, and he is, or says he is, the first to understand the "point" about the cogwheel (29), and he never tires of telling his listeners about the way in which his bright ideas arrive. However, when he lists the lessons he has drawn from his experiences (49), most of them are patently wrong! It seems that the inherited gifts, the ability to make judgments, and the self-criticism of which he boasts at an early stage have weaknesses of which he is unaware.

Whether the irony over Pappa's falling into the water, referred to above, is to be seen as stemming from him or the author is not entirely clear, but as he seems in general to possess remarkably little sense of humor at his own expense, it must presumably come from the author who has created him. The same irony is also to be found in the passionate, declamatory, even melodramatic style that Pappa employs about himself. At times he sounds almost Byronic:

> Hiding my face in my hands, I sighed, "Alone! Cruel World! Fate is my Destiny!"--and other sad expressions, until I felt a little better. (3)

Not only is the entire scene portrayed in an ironical light, but the irony is twofold, as Pappa is naive enough to talk of speaking in these terms "until he felt a little better." It is as though he both sees himself as a tragic figure and yet at the same time feels he can help himself on his way. The Byronic outbursts are not limited to the early part of the book, but continue, as do his allusions to the idea of Fate. Indeed, taken as a whole, his view seems to be that he is fated to be something great. Not everyone shares his view, and when he rhapsodically talks to Hodgkins in such terms and tells him that he is a fugitive born under special stars, Hodgkins innocently but devastatingly asks under which stars. Instead of understanding the implication of the question, Pappa gives him a long explanation and feels grateful for at last finding someone who will listen to him. His previous attempts at telling his life story to captive audiences have been doomed to failure, as most of the creatures he has met in the forest have been too busy to listen. Hodgkins does listen, but he is inclined to understatement and lacks effusiveness, with the consequence that Pappa, for the sake of his own ego, is constrained to interpret Hodgkins's words when he merely remarks that Pappa's house looks quite good:

> He said it was a good house. (Thereby he meant that it was a wonderful and fascinating house. Hodgkins never cared much for big words.) (21) [26]

Pappa does, of course, sometimes literally speak with capital letters in his text.

There is yet another instance when the reader is not sure whether he is laughing at or with Pappa. It is the occasion when he sets out in the darkness to save someone in distress. When he has carried out his heroic deed, it emerges that he has saved a hemulen who is virtually indistinguishable from the principal of the orphanage from which he fled. The episode is told in heroic tones, with Pappa making a great show of the efforts he expended, but the result is a carefully engineered anticlimax. The rescue is recounted in bombastic tones, with Pappa asking that a granite monument representing two weeping hemulens (!) be raised in memory of him if he should not return. In the end, of course, he effects the rescue and returns to the houseboat, only to wish he had never undertaken the foolhardy trip. His reaction on discovering whom he has rescued is a reversion to his childhood habits, and he raises his tail to the obligatory 45 degrees before remembering that he is a "free" moomintroll.

The Groke, from whom he rescues the hemulen, is here described at her most fearsome. There is always something menacing about the Groke, at least until Moomintroll manages to establish some kind of contact with her in <u>Moominpappa at Sea</u>, but normally the menace is unspecified. Here she is said actually to eat people, and the accompanying illustration shows a Groke who looks terrifying indeed, with an outsize hand reaching over the mountain, vicious teeth in a large mouth, an outsize nose, and staring eyes. Either the "mountains" are very small, or she is inordinately large. Yet the question remains, of course, whether Pappa's account of the entire event is trustworthy, or whether it is another example of his improving on details, as he admits he does. The reader is left with the conviction that the end of this adventure is a fiasco, but with the suspicion that the whole thing was perhaps less heroic than the account seems to indicate. It is not entirely without parallel, either: when Pappa is visited by the ghost, he does the obvious thing and hides--yet, looking back, he decides that he was not really afraid and explains that he went very <u>determinedly</u> under the bed!

In this story Pappa emerges as a self-important person whose pompousness is tempered by his naivete. He becomes so transparent in his conceit that the reader actually likes him, and he thus becomes more than a mere type, more than a mere representation of a single human characteristic. He is in fact a complex figure whose complexities nevertheless cannot conceivably confuse the child reader. And it must still be remembered that this is a children's book. He is the hero who endears himself to the children through his very weakness, and the game of distinguishing between truth and fiction is left to the more skeptical adult reader.

**Secondary Characters**

Little is seen of Mamma in this story, though she does appear, as it were, on two levels. At the very end, she makes her entrance into Pappa's life when, heroic as usual, he saves her from the waves. Nevertheless, she is true to her nature as we already know it, the rather proper figure looking for her handbag like a medieval housewife for her keys--though in this case she wants the facepowder the handbag contains so she can make herself look respectable after her ordeal. However, this brief portrayal is balanced by the occasional glimpse of her in the interludes, when she attends to the comfort of the family and listens to Pappa reading his work aloud. She can be radiant at the prospect of appearing in the story herself. The cynic would note, however, that despite Pappa's kind words about her, the part she plays is incredibly small. Pappa's meeting with her <u>can</u> be seen as the climax of the whole story (and Pappa seems to hint at this)--but it can also represent the moment when he lost his newly found and much lauded independence!

At all events, Pappa obviously feels most at ease with warm, stable, straightforward characters such as Hodgkins and Mamma. There is a greater distance between him and the other principal figures in the story. His dislike of the hemulen, straight-laced, domineering, and unimaginative, is unmistakable, explicit, and consistent. On the other hand, he is tolerant toward the Joxter, the happy-go-lucky Bohemian, and the restless, selfish Muddler. That these two figures have a particular function in Tove Jansson's work seems to be indicated by the fact that they are later paralleled by Snufkin and Sniff, their respective offspring. The family likeness is apparent from Tove Jansson's illustrations. A third type, also duplicated, is the Mymble's daughter, whose impudent sister Little My often happily keeps Pappa from too extravagant flights of fancy in the later work.

This novel, then, seems to center on one figure who is more than a personification of a single human attribute, surrounded by others whose characteristics are simpler: bourgeois respectability, selfishness, calm indifference to the world. In the background there are the hattifatteners who represent the deeper, primitive urges in human nature, and the Groke, who here is seen as a fairly tangible threat to her fellow creatures. It is an adventure story, and the adventures in themselves imply a lack of security, danger in everyday life, with the storm at sea reminiscent of that in <u>Finn Family Moomintroll</u> and others in the series. The theme of a violent storm and a visit to an island is a persistent element in Tove Jansson's work.

The question inevitably again arises as to whether this is a children's book or not. Much of it will be accessible to children. The picaresque element, the series of more or less connected adventures, fits in well with a good deal of children's literature, and many of the adventures are intelligible to a child. Yet even in these individual episodes, there are details that are reserved for the grown-up. The visit to Daddy Jones's park contains various episodes of a simple, amusing nature, and the search for eggs and the distribution of prizes at the end will doubtless appeal to the unsophisticated imagination. However, the prize awarded to Pappa will attract the adult imagination more, and the adult might well ask whether this really has the profound significance that Pappa himself ascribes to it. <u>Is</u> it the best? Or is Pappa merely trying to maintain his position? The choice is left to the reader.

## Chapter Six
# *Moominsummer Madness*

Four years elapsed between <u>The Exploits of Moominpappa</u> and Tove Jansson's next Moomin book, <u>Moominsummer Madness</u>. The mixture of styles was scarcely the same in the new book. The picaresque nature of the previous novels was radically changed, though not, perhaps, entirely abandoned. There <u>is</u> still a journey from one adventure to another, though it now bears only a slight resemblance to the series of adventures occasioned by the magician's hat or the journey through life contained in <u>The Exploits of Moominpappa</u>. In this case the family is forced to leave its home because of a great flood caused by a volcanic eruption. In the course of its involuntary journey in a new, floating "house"--in fact, a theater floating on the floodwaters--Moomintroll and the Snork Maiden decide to spend a night in a tree, only to find their "home" has vanished during the night, and Little My falls into the water and disappears. After various adventures, the family is reunited and returns to Moomin Valley.

The great difference between this plot and those of the earlier books, however, is that this is not a simple story of the unrelated adventures that occur during a journey, but rather a carefully dovetailed series of adventures in which no episode is superfluous and every event carries significance for the ultimate happy ending. <u>The Exploits of Moominpappa</u> ended almost like a show, or a somewhat unconvincing and artificial party, with all the cast gathered together to take a bow. This book brings them together in a highly organized and convincing manner, and curiously enough literally on a stage.

### A Complex Plot

The story begins idyllically, with Mamma sitting sunning herself and making a toy boat for Moomintroll, though the threat to the idyll quickly becomes apparent, when soot falls from a volcano in the distance.

## Moominsummer Madness

Snufkin has not yet returned from his winter wanderings, though it is very late in the year for him, and Moomintroll in particular misses him. Suddenly the volcano erupts violently, the earth cracks, and during the night, the waters in the valley rise and completely engulf the lower story of the Moomin house. The family withdraws to the upper floors, but as the waters rise still faster, they are relieved to see what they think is a floating house, and they take refuge in it. It does not take the reader long to discover that it is in fact a floating theater, but Tove Jansson here enjoys herself as she tells of the Moomin family's misunderstanding: they do not know what a theater is. They make contact with a rat called Emma, who appears to have been a kind of factotum in the theater and is at first antagonistic to the new occupants.

It is at this juncture that the simple story becomes more complex, partly because Emma deliberately sets the theater adrift when Moomintroll and the Snork Maiden decide to camp out for the night--a piece of treachery which is never discovered--and partly because of Little My's disappearance. Ensconced in a sewing basket, she is washed down the river, but is finally caught by Snufkin, who is angling at the riverside. Although he does not recognize her, he puts her in his pocket and looks after her. She is thus caught up in a scheme of his, which is to take his revenge on a park keeper (park keepers have already been seen to be among his favorite aversions). They go to the park and sow some hattifattener seeds on the lawns; when these seeds quickly develop into hattifatteners (something only possible on midsummer eve) the terrified park keeper and his wife flee the place, thus giving Snufkin the opportunity to pull down all the notices saying "No . . ."

Meanwhile, Moomintroll and the Snork Maiden have wandered through the forest and come to a house occupied by a lonely fillyjonk, who according to tradition has invited her uncle and his wife to celebrate midsummer eve together with her, though from past experience she knows perfectly well that will not come. So Moomintroll and the Snork Maiden decide to celebrate it with her instead; in their search for something with which to make a bonfire they find a lot of notice boards lying around. They burn them and then go out gathering flowers. Upon looking into the water to see the image of the person they are to marry, they find instead the reflection of a hemulen policeman, who arrests them for having taken down the notice boards and burned them.

While all this is going on, Pappa has decided to write a play, putting it, on orders from Emma, into hexameters. The play is advertised, and all the local animals decide to attend. The hemulen policeman wants to go as well, and he leaves his three prisoners in the hands of his kindly but rather simple cousin. She promptly takes them home to tea and not only allows them to escape but herself goes to the theater with them. There she discovers that Emma is her long lost uncle's wife, a fact that the reader has long suspected, thanks to a "photograph" which is reproduced by Tove Jansson in the text.

As a result of his adventures in the park, Snufkin finds himself surrounded by twenty-four tiny children who treat him as their father--an experience that the peace-loving Snufkin scarcely enjoys. They find a deserted house--belonging, of course, to the fillyjonk--and there they find the program for the theater performance. But in their eagerness they tear it to shreds, so that parts of it are illegible, thereby ensuring that Snufkin learns about the performance without discovering who is responsible for it. They go to the performance and are reunited with the Moomin family, though the arrival of Moomintroll and company is marred by the hemulen policeman's attempt to rearrest them. Snufkin now admits the crime but escapes, followed by the Moomin family plus the hemulen's cousin who busily but unimaginatively sets about writing out the five thousand lines that are the punishment for the crime. The family now approaches Moomin Valley, where the water is subsiding. They are captured by the police, however, and Snufkin is about to be led away when the cousin turns up and hands in the lines, at which point Snufkin is set free, having promised not to do such a dastardly thing again. The family is now reunited, and Moomintroll finds the boat his mother had made for him before the adventure began. The first thing she does is to finish the dinghy she had originally forgotten to make for it. The idyll is restored.

**Implications**

Technically, the novel is superior to the earlier ones, heralding Tove Jansson's later writing. On the other hand, the technical dexterity, with its elements of mystery and excitement, still gives the story that element of suspense that belongs to a children's book, and although none of Tove Jansson's books can be said to be devoid of adult interest, there is less of interest here for an adult than there was in The Exploits of Moominpappa. The overtones are largely missing, and the characters are portrayed on a more superficial level: Pappa, for instance, has become a shadowy figure, though as always he retains his basic characteristics. More than any of the earlier stories, this novel exists by dint of the action.

Nevertheless, there are aspects here of greater interest to adults, or adults are more likely than children to discover them, but they tend to be details rather than major themes. There is, for instance, the drama. It surely can be thoroughly appreciated only by an adult. Naturally, children will laugh with the children in the story at the antics of the lion on the stage. But few children will understand Pappa's problem in writing hexameters. Nor will children appreciate the element of pastiche in the rhetorical, high-flown drama of which only the outlines and a couple of extracts are shown. This will be lost on them--as it is lost on the audience in the book. This gathering of small animals who have come to see Pappa's great drama has not the slightest idea of what it is about. However, when Little My turns up, climbs onto the stage, and causes a general disturbance, both the fictional audience and the child reader will decide that the boisterous reunion is far better than the poetical tragedy they have just witnessed. Now they understand the drama being enacted: "It was about someone who had floated away from home and had awful experiences and now found her way home again" (129) [128]. If the reader is to draw any lesson from this, it is that everyday drama is more likely to win a hearing and meet with understanding than high-flown romantic rhetoric. In this way, the novel can be seen as a defense of everyday reality.

Certainly that reality is at the center of the book, together with the security and comfort that go with it, the warmth of everyday human relations. It starts with idyll, and it ends with idyll. It starts with Mamma looking after the family's needs, and it ends with her doing exactly the same. Throughout the tribulations encountered by the family, Mamma does her best to maintain the atmosphere of a home, seeing to everyone's needs, providing for their comfort, doing her best to cook the family's food in strange new surroundings. She tries, within the compass of the theater in which they take refuge, to re-create something of the atmosphere of the original home to which they long to return. Yet their new "home" is, despite familiar aspects, no longer the one they have known, and the description of it amidst the stage furniture is a clever piece of writing hinting at the unknown and at accompanying danger:

> The table looked a little lonely in the large and unfamiliar room. The chairs, the looking-glass cabinet, and the linen cupboard kept watch around it, but behind them lurked an expanse of darkness, silence and dust. The ceiling, from which the drawing-room lamp should have hung securely with its fringe of red tassels, the ceiling was the strangest of all. It was lost in mysterious, moving and fluttering shadows, while something large and vague kept slowly rocking to and fro with the house's movements in the water.
> "There's a lot of things one can't understand," Moominmamma said to herself. "But why should everything be exactly as one is used to having it?" (38) [36]

There are ominous overtones in this passage, clearly denoting the unknown dangers besetting the family when it is taken out of its accustomed surroundings. By analogy, this can be extended to the plight of humanity when in a state of disarray. Likewise, Mamma's final remark that there is so much that she does not understand, together with her recognition that everything will continue unchanged, can certainly be taken at more than face value. The book was published in 1954, at a time when the world was undergoing great changes; what seemed to be familiar surroundings were beset by the unknown with its concomitant dangers. To this extent, then, the novel is an allegory: "All the world's a stage"! While Mamma and Pappa try to re-create their lost home, the other members of the group leave the immediate security and try to explore the new reality surrounding them. While Mamma is looking for jam to give her family, the Whomper goes exploring in the dark recesses of the stage, where he meets the Mymble's daughter. Likewise Misabel and the Snork Maiden go exploring and each finds what she is looking for, in the one case, wigs and in the other, dresses. Dangers there may be, but this unknown territory has something to offer those who venture into it instead of Mamma's philosophizing.

A clear distinction is drawn in this novel between the Moomin family and outsiders, and it is perhaps in this book that Tove Jansson for the first time introduces what might be termed a social perspective into her work. In all essentials the Moomin family is middle class and respectable, despite Pappa's urge to break out, and they represent stability and comfort and appreciate the security of their home in Moomin Valley. They are subjected to many adventures in the course of the Moomin books, but there is no doubt in anyone's mind that they would rather most of them had not happened. Pappa might or might not be a born adventurer, but he certainly has adapted to a family situation that does not approve of such a characteristic. The crisis resulting from this comes finally in <u>Moominpappa at Sea</u>.

The other characters can be divided into two broad groups: those who in one way or another are straight-laced and unimaginative, such as the hemulens, and the group that wants to break with normal conventions, such as Snufkin and more ephemeral characters like Misabel. The question arises as to whether this group is socially different. The answer is yes.

The theme is not really developed, though it does recur. To Mamma's consternation, the Whomper reacts sharply to the suggestion that it is only scoundrels who fare ill, while Misabel at one stage feels herself to be the poor relation; the difference in her dress and looks is underlined by the drawing of her together with the Snork Maiden and the Mymble's daughter (46). The mixture of self-righteousness and envy appropriate to the situation is then underlined by what she says to the others:

> "You and your old fluff!" she cried out, bursting into tears. "You know everything, don't you! And the Snork Maiden hasn't even got a frock on! I'd

never never never show myself if I weren't properly dressed! I'd sooner be <u>dead</u> than have no frock on!" (50) [47]

For his part, the Whomper underlines what he sees as a lack of initiative and curiosity on the part of the Moomins; he considers them to be more sensitive than he is, but far less interested in questioning their surroundings, a comment that is interesting in view of Pappa's rather vague philosophizing in <u>The Exploits of Moominpappa</u> and <u>Moominpappa at Sea</u>:

> "They're all so very unlike me," he thought. "They have feelings and they see colours and hear sounds and whirl around, but <u>what</u> they feel and see and hear, and <u>why</u> they whirl doesn't concern them in the least." (47) [44]

And this is true: the revolving stage causes no consternation, and when the lights at the edge of the stage go on with the fall of darkness, Mámma simply accepts this as a matter of course, something that ensures security to the family:

> "That's to prevent people from falling in the water," said Moominmamma. "How orderly life can be." (48) [44]

Ultimately, then, her horizon is as limited as that of any of the other characters, but her limitations in this field are combined with warmth and a care for others. It is symptomatic that Snufkin with his twenty-four children automatically and longingly assumes that Mamma will take care of them when he finds her.

### New Elements

In practice, of course, the children go to the fillyjonk, who represents one of Tove Jansson's first studies in loneliness. Whatever the reason, the fillyjonk is a lonely, neglected person. She is a pitiful creature when first seen, dressed for a party, with a bell on her cap, well knowing that the guests are not going to come, and when Moomintroll and the Snork Maiden turn up, she realizes that for once, indeed for the first time in her life, she is really going to have a midsummer party. When she goes picking flowers with the Snork Maiden, the illustrations show her still dressed in a jester's garb, but the face is that of a sad jester.

In a curious way, the drama of the real Moomin life is removed to the stage in <u>Moominsummer Madness</u>. The idyll is disturbed by a tangible event, the volcano, but there is no real menace sensed in this, no real danger to the family. The elements that usually constitute a menace to their existence are scarcely a threat in this case. The Groke is mentioned in passing but is not seen: indeed, she is reduced to a mere threat to naughty children. The hattifatteners are no longer related to dissoluteness nor are they even a mysterious presence; here they are simply a source of amusement. The electric charges that are used to instill an element of fear in other novels are here used to provide fun. Yet, as already seen, there are unknown areas in the theater which for a time at least cause apprehension, and Emma, who finally turns out to be a harmless though somewhat bad-tempered creature, for a time acts as an unseen and unknown threat, a creature who eats the family's food, utters threatening or disgusted laughs, and is directly responsible for marooning Moomintroll and the Snork Maiden. To a large extent, life is lived on the stage, and for some of the characters at least the stage becomes a fulfillment. Misabel, who goes through life in tragic postures, weeping over the slightest thing, is finally able to fulfill herself in a tragic role. The Whomper too finds ample outlet for his inquisitiveness. The Snork Maiden also finds sufficient scope for her vanity, though she finally leaves together with the rest of the family. The Mymble's daughter, aggressive as always, wants to be the instrument for helping Misabel to her tragic end, but she is not given this honor. The Whomper, of course, is disappointed that Pappa's drama is not a detective play.

With <u>Moominsummer Madness</u>, the Moomin books are firmly established in a new pattern. But it is not a set pattern. It leaves room for development both of intrigue and character portrayal, and the remainder of the series shows how Tove Jansson now moves freely within the framework she has set herself.

## Chapter Seven
# *Moominland Midwinter*

While the earlier books in one way or another were dominated by action, an action extending over a lengthy time or a considerable area, the emphasis is different in <u>Moominland Midwinter</u>. Here character is stressed rather than action, and the author clearly begins to consider the question of the nature of reality. The action as such centers on a situation rather than an elaborate story, and Tove Jansson is concerned with a series of individual events and a unique situation that together illustrate a radical development in the nature of Moomintroll. If the book were to be considered exclusively from an adult point of view, it could be described as a novel of character, a psychological novel with philosophical overtones. Perhaps the only thing that prevents its being conclusively classed as such is that its premises are still fundamentally those of the children's book: the Moomin world, the fantasy characters that inhabit it, and the memory of the earlier books which play a part in creating the basis on which this novel is built.

### The Theme of Change

The unique character of the action is directly indicated when the reader is told that Moomintroll, in wakening from his hibernation before the winter has passed, has done something never known before, and his vain efforts to waken his mother in the first chapter underline that this is indeed a most unusual occurrence. Moomintroll is alone--almost alone--in a sleeping house, and not unnaturally he moves into the snow-covered world outside where he is confronted with a sight different from anything he has seen before. At first he is intensely lonely, but Little My, hibernating in a cave, is awakened by a confused and forgetful squirrel looking for something warm to sleep on. Before she and Moomintroll find each other, however, Moomintroll meets someone he has never seen before, a creature with more human features than most of the other characters in the Moomin books, Too-ticky, who becomes his mentor throughout his winter adventures. Too-ticky takes him to his own bathhouse, where he is looked after by her and some invisible shrews; she warns him of the bitter cold approaching in the shape of an ice maiden and shows him a horse she has made of snow. As the coldest time of the winter approaches, other small creatures appear on the scene, brought to Moomin Valley by rumors that there is food in the Moomin House. At first Moomintroll is inclined to defend his mother's provisions, but in the end, he opens the house and the larder, and the "guests" take possession. The squirrel, forgetful as ever, fails to keep out of the way of the ice maiden and dies of cold, after which he is carried off on the snow horse. Moomintroll goes so far as to allow some of the old furniture to be burned on a midwinter bonfire--which is subsequently extinguished by the Groke.

One of the mysteries of the winter scene has been the presence of some creature in the bathhouse. It lives in a cupboard, which Moomintroll is told by Too-ticky not to open. But he does, of course, and discovers a tiny creature, faintly resembling himself, with whom he cannot establish contact, but who is said to be his "ancestor." The "ancestor" finally takes refuge in the stove in the Moominhouse. (It will be remembered that Moomins used to live in stoves, and that this has determined the shape of the houses they build.) The relative peace and comfort of the winter gathering in the Moomin house is spoiled by the arrival of a hemulen. He is well-intentioned, but like all hemulens, without sensitivity or imagination, and he drives both Moomintroll and the otherwise incredibly patient Too-ticky almost to despair, so much so that they entice him away with the prospect of better skiing terrain in the Lonely Mountains. He leaves, accompanied by one of the tiny creatures staying in the house: despite her enticing name of Salome she has been ignored by the others but has become devoted to the hemulen. He is also followed by the little dog, Sorry-oo, who has fancied himself a descendant of the wolves, until he encounters them and discovers a more menacing band of relatives than he likes.

At the end of the winter the guests depart, and Mamma awakens--somewhat earlier than usual--in time to see the ice break up and the snow melt. With her usual patience and fortitude she accepts the disarray in the house and the disappearance of the jam she had stored over the months. Little My, daring as ever, goes skating on the ice as it breaks up and has to be rescued by Moomintroll. Finally Snufkin returns with the advent of spring, and Moomintroll is reunited with his closest friend. On the surface, at least, much is as it was before.

But only on the surface. By means of a widespread use of symbols and associations, Tove Jansson has invested her story of the mysterious goings-on in the winter with an allegorical presentation of radical change. She is concerned with portraying the change from unconscious childhood to conscious childhood; the further change from childhood to incipient adulthood is to come later in <u>Moominpappa at Sea</u>. The transformation here is brought about by giving Moomintroll insight into a world that has hitherto been unknown to him, although it has always existed. Instead of depicting a gradual dawn of understanding such as that experienced by a normal human being, she confronts him with the entire reality of a new situation and shows him gradually coming to terms with it. The story of <u>Moominland Midwinter</u> is the story of Moomintroll's awakening consciousness and his emergence from unenquiring childhood. In traditional style he needs a mentor, Too-ticky, who guides him through the mysteries of the winter rather like a Beatrice, though she has a somewhat more passive role and limits herself to guiding only when necessary and not always giving the information or understanding that Moomintroll seeks. Perhaps one of her chief functions is <u>not</u> to give him answers, but to help him understand that his previous reality is not the only reality. When at a very early stage he talks of the bathhouse as belonging to his father, she answers him in terms which he does not immediately understand, but which in fact are unambiguous: "'You might be right and you might be wrong,' she said. 'In the summer it belonged to a daddy. In winter it belongs to Too-ticky'" (28) [24]. The place is the same, the surroundings are the same, but the reality is different, and what Moomintroll until now has been able to take as undifferentiated truth becomes a relative truth in his new existence. Even time is relative: Moomintroll sets all the clocks in the house going but at different times on the supposition that at least one of them is likely to be right. Which one is a matter of indifference. (The question of the relativity of time is taken up again in The Doll's House from 1978.)

**The Question of Reality**

This move from the absolute to the relative typifies the transition that is fundamental to the novel. The absolute and unquestioned reality of the world of childhood now becomes less clearly defined, something a growing Moomintroll can question. Likewise, Moomintroll, who has hitherto been protected, now learns to live without that protection, a development that is betokened at the end of the book when the Snork Maiden wants to cover a crocus in order to protect it from the cold but is stopped by Moomintroll, whose new view is that it must manage on its own: "Let it fight it out. I believe it's going to do still better if things aren't so easy" (137) [131]. He could not have uttered these words at the beginning of the book, and they represent the sum of his experience in this winter of change. They are moreover almost a repetition of something Too-ticky has said to him: when spring is returning, he asks her why she has not told him that the winter would pass, at which she shrugs her shoulders and remarks that one has to discover everything for oneself and get over it all on one's own (119) [113].

It is not from choice that Moomintroll makes his discoveries: the process of growing up is an involuntary one that cannot be stopped; therefore he cannot go to sleep again once he has awakened from his hibernation. He moves into the unknown, and until he meets Too-ticky he is completely on his own. Such moves as he makes are to look back, and in fact, there are throughout numerous instances of his natural tendency to look back on what he has known but has lost. The very first thing he does is to read Snufkin's spring letter, the greeting he had written for him before leaving in October; it is a greeting from the past, a promise to return with the spring, and a symbol of contact with Snufkin, with whom Moomintroll is closely associated. In his way, Snufkin represents a more disorderly form of security than that represented by Mamma and Pappa, and after Moomintroll has experienced snow for the first time and seen the Lonely Mountains as a desolate, cold landscape, his first thoughts are of Snufkin, "sitting somewhere in the sun, peeling an orange" (23) [19]. One might almost think he has read Goethe! He continues to find comfort in familiar things, and he fixes glossy pictures of summer with its flowers and its sunshine onto the walls of the snow-covered Moomin house--though it is significant that the pictures are described as reminding him of the world he has lost, a double entendre that will not escape the observant reader (35). For a considerable time, it is what he has lost that represents reality for him:

> "Here one comes stumbling into something altogether new and strange, and not a soul even asking one in what kind of world one has lived before. Not even Little My wants to talk about the real world."
> "And how does one tell which one is the real one?" said Too-ticky. (45) [40]

Tove Jansson does not go so far as to deny the reality of Moomintroll's childhood world, but she is asking whether it is the only one. She asks a similar question in more dramatic form in The Doll's House.

At all events Moomintroll cannot return to his lost paradise, and his first reaction is one of longing to return but with the realization that this is not possible:

> "I don't belong here any more," Moomintroll thought. "Nor there. I don't even know what's waking and what's a dream." And then in an instant he was asleep, and summer lilacs covered him in their friendly green shadow. (31) [27]

The summer that has been his reality is now only his dream; everything connected with the summer, the whole of his family life, is part of a sleeping world from which he is now excluded. His task is not to long back to it, but to come to terms with the new reality in which he finds himself.

In its way, even the new winter presents questions of reality. The new smell reaching Moomintroll's nostrils may well be "more serious" (a striking expression to use of a smell), but a distinction is drawn between what he sees and therefore expects to experience and what he actually does experience. It is, for instance, late in the book that he realizes that the snow covering the earth has fallen from the skies and that it is not something like grass that grows up from the soil. The real situation has been outside his experience so far. On a different level, there is the question of Too-ticky's snow horse, which is made of snow and yet not what it seems to be--and Moomintroll gives it a wide berth. Is it snow, or is it a horse? The story seems to imply that it is both--or neither--that reality is something indeterminate. The relativity of reality is also clearly implied in the visit to the bathhouse. Even before Too-ticky specifically says that what is his father's in the summer is hers in the winter, Moomintroll has sensed something unknown. "Everything was exactly as in summer. But still the room had changed in some mysterious way" (27) [23]. That he is immediately told not to open the cupboard in which his blue dressing gown hangs compounds his sense of a change, though he significantly refuses to promise not to look inside it. When he finally does so, it is a sign that Moomintroll, who has been the docile child of his mother, is no longer prepared to defer to others, that he is developing a will of his own, a defiance of others that is completely new to him.

The question of appearance and reality, of understanding and not understanding, stretches well beyond this stage. The novel contains more than its usual share of strange creatures, though many of them are sensed rather than seen. There are the invisible shrews who wait on Too-ticky in the bathhouse; there is the strange pair of eyes Moomintroll sees under the chest of drawers in the sitting room, and which he never quite identifies; and there is his "ancestor," who appears from a cupboard to which Moomintroll is accustomed to going and disappears into the stove, after which he is not seen again. Then there are the strange animals, who come to the midwinter bonfire, heralded by Too-ticky in a song. What these creatures are is never made clear, as they are only seen from a distance, either in the light of the torches they are carrying or in the light from the bonfire.

There is an almost ritual significance to the midwinter bonfire, which is lit by Too-ticky, and the entire ceremony appears to signify the winter world (in a symbolical sense therefore the adult world) in which

Moomintroll does not yet feel at home. Such is the indeterminate nature of these beings, the obvious cultic manner in which they are used, the distance at which they are kept. Their elusive nature is such that the reader, at least the adult reader, might well be forgiven for wondering whether they are really supposed to exist at all or whether they are to be understood as fantasies in Moomintroll's developing imagination.

**Warmth and Understanding**

Part of Moomintroll's experience on this night is his first close look at the Groke, whereby the midwinter bonfire assumes a new significance, as his subsequent urge to make contact with the Groke appears to stem from it. Hitherto, she has been a figure of fear, but here she emerges as a pitiful if not entirely sympathetic figure, a nuisance to others, but a creature ultimately looking for warmth--by which the adult reader will understand more than the literal warmth of the bonfire which she promptly proceeds to dowse:

> "Take it easy," replied Too-ticky. "She didn't come to extinguish the fire, you see, she came to warm herself, poor creature. But everything that's warm goes cold when she sits down on it. Now she's disappointed once more." (63) [58]

And the Groke moves off in silent disappointment.

In itself, this encounter with the Groke, in which Moomintroll is presented with her reality rather than the myth he has known before, can be seen as a movement toward greater understanding, tolerance, and warmth, a movement that achieves its objective in <u>Moominpappa at Sea</u>. Nor is the Groke the only creature to call on Moomintroll's warmer feelings. The idyll that he and his guests have established is seriously disturbed by the arrival of the hemulen. His insistence on blowing a horn, his garment of yellow jersey with zigzag black stripes, and his enthusiasm for interesting others in the outdoor life are sufficient to make Moomintroll-- and even Too-ticky--reach the conclusion that somehow or other they must get rid of him for their own comfort and that of everyone else. The otherwise placid and tolerant Too-ticky says outright that he must be told to go, to which Moomintroll originally reacts by saying that he cannot be hardhearted enough to do it: the hemulen thinks everyone likes him, and he cannot bring himself to disillusion him. Moreover, Moomintroll, who has now experienced loneliness himself, sees signs of it in the hemulen and decides at least to try to get rid of him without his realizing it. So the plan is devised to fire him with enthusiasm for better skiing grounds and send him to the Lonely Mountains, despite the fact that they are known to be dangerous. Moomintroll gets up enough courage to do this--but immediately regrets it and persuades the hemulen to stay. His better self and his sense of responsibility overcome what is a selfish if natural reaction. It is scarcely by chance at this stage, when he has really overcome many of his selfish, childish attitudes, that he thinks that perhaps winter is not so bad after all. His acceptance of winter represents his acceptance of the conditions into which he has no choice but to grow. He goes so far as to sacrifice his prized pot of strawberry jam to the hemulen; he even tells him he wants to learn to ski, though his one experience of it was catastrophic and significantly made him long for home.

The jam Moomintroll gives to the hemulen has been hidden in the stove, the symbol of the primitive stage of the Moomintrolls and the hiding place of the "ancestor," in other words, a symbol of the past. In taking the pot of jam out of the stove and giving it to the hemulen, Moomintroll is symbolizing the way in which he is committing himself to the present and turning his back on a sentimental worship of the past. He does, admittedly, also look for his "ancestor," but, he thinks, "things that happen now really <u>are</u> more interesting than those that happened a thousand years ago" (108) [103]. What is happening now is an act of generosity, a sign of warm feelings and kindness for those alive now.

Yet another sign of the innate warmth and understanding expressed by the book as a whole is the hemulen's attitude toward Salome, the tiny neglected creature who adores him. She has heard the plans for enticing the hemulen away, and she is afraid for him; a snowstorm comes on, and she goes to look for him, only to find no trace of him. She naturally assumes that he has gone away and sets off to find him, but becomes lost in the snow. When this becomes apparent, it is the hemulen who goes off to find her; he has little sense of having neglected her, no bad conscience--"hemulens seldom have that"--but nevertheless, something impels him to look for her. He finds her, and when he finally goes off, she goes with him. This is the most positive portrayal of a hemulen so far in Tove Jansson's work; this horn-blowing, ski fiend is very far from the prim and proper hemulen to whom Pappa owed his early upbringing, far, too, from the kindly but rather unintelligent little hemulen who allowed the party to escape in <u>Moominsummer Madness</u>. The inevitable conclusion is that hemulens are not creatures with great perspectives or sensitivities, but that within limits, they are a varied group.

The other figure who goes off with the hemulen is Sorry-oo, the tiny and somewhat woebegone dog who thinks he is related to the wolves and wants to go back to his distant relatives. The instinct that drags him in that direction is perhaps a kind of parallel to that which draws Moomintroll toward his ancestor, and in the end both are seen to be romantic dreams. Moomintroll gives up his ancestor without realizing it, but Sorry-oo has to face reality in a different way, going out to howl in the darkness, until one day the wolves actually do come and show themselves to be very different from what he had imagined. They are never really seen, but their eyes shine in the darkness as they draw nearer and are ready to snap up the miserable dog. He is saved at the last moment by the arrival of the horn-blowing hemulen. <u>He</u> at any rate has no imagination and is unlikely to get lost in the kind of daydreaming in which Sorry-oo has indulged.

**My and Too-ticky**

Meanwhile, the hemulen has not in fact been the only creature present who has little sense of atmosphere and very little interest in anything but himself. The other is Little My, though she is so small she can scarcely create much disturbance. In a way she is a foil to Moomintroll, for like him she is awakened at the beginning of the winter and has to learn to cope with a world she has not known before. However, she learns very quickly. She is a creature who can deal with any situation, at a very early stage discovering that Mamma's silver tray makes an excellent toboggan and then becoming an expert skier and later a proficient skater. In contrast to Moomintroll, she never panics and is never overcome by regret at having lost the world she has known. One of her functions is to bring Moomintroll back to earth when he becomes too abstract and unrealistic.

It can be argued that while Little My represents an impish, possibly even an egotistical desire to keep the Troll in reality, Too-ticky represents a conscious desire to guide him toward an independent acceptance of the new reality. She philosophizes and sometimes points to the moral; she is always there for Moomintroll to turn to when he is either perplexed or in need. In that sense, she takes the place of Mamma, who sleeps throughout virtually the whole book. But she does not replace Mamma's protectiveness; on the contrary, she deliberately fosters Moomintroll's independence and his ability to cope, often merely shrugging her shoulders or making remarks to the effect that it cannot be helped, that is how things are. When the spring returns, and Moomintroll realizes that the world he has known before is also a part of reality and that in a sense it is returning, he reproaches Too-ticky for not having comforted him by telling him that the winter would pass. At this point she says that he had to discover things for himself and learn to manage on his own without the knowledge that things would come right in the end. It is this moral Moomintroll points to the Snork Maiden when she wants to protect her crocus.

Too-ticky can be tolerant, but she can be equally firm and even stern at times; moreover she clearly points to the limits of knowledge, whereby she once more implies the uncertain nature of reality. She goes so far as to seek to explain the existence of death when Moomintroll for the first time in his life is confronted with it and finds it a distressing experience:

> "When one's dead, then one's dead," said Too-ticky kindly. "This squirrel will become earth all in his time. And still later on there'll grow trees from him, with new squirrels skipping about in them. Do you think that's so very sad?" (49) [44]

This neat definition of the life cycle with its implication that living things decompose and in so doing provide the basis for new life will satisfy the adult reader, but here a slight gesture is made to the sensitivities of the child. There is a footnote referring to a later page when, in the spring, Moomintroll sees a squirrel that looks exactly like this one. Asked whether it is the same one, the squirrel cannot remember. The adult will realize that it is <u>not</u> the same one, but the child reader will be satisfied and, perhaps, comforted. The truth can be presented in more than one way, and the squirrel's innate forgetfulness is put to good effect.

Too-ticky understands many things, but in particular it is her task to guide Moomintroll to a new reality. He has known one reality and now adapts to another, thus giving the book a double perspective. Moomintroll changes even if not completely, and reality becomes a less clearly defined concept. These two themes--change and the definition of reality--are, of course, closely related, and they become essential features of most of Tove Jansson's work from now onward.

## Chapter Eight
# *Tales from Moomin Valley*

<u>Moominland Midwinter</u> heralded a change of course in Tove Jansson's writing, and her next major publication, <u>Tales from Moomin Valley</u>, was to confirm it. It is again a more profound study of personality than the earlier works, less tied to a linear action. It is a series of short stories, a genre that her adult work is largely, though not exclusively, based upon. The episodic nature of her early works indicates a natural tendency in this direction even then.

"The Spring Tune," the first of these stories, is on the surface a study of Snufkin, who has been seen intermittently in the novels so far, usually appearing in the spring and leaving with the approach of winter. He has stood as the type of the independent individualist, the wanderer who knows no ties, gentle, well liked, but something of an enigma.

However, whereas he has hitherto been seen from the outside--as have most of the other figures as well--he is seen here as a personality in his own right. He becomes the central figure in a short story showing him in a completely different light. He is first seen in the forest, trying to compose a spring tune, but the tune has a life of its own and will not quite come until the right moment. Snufkin thinks briefly of Moomintroll, who will be expecting his arrival, but he dismisses him quickly from his mind so as not to disturb the inspiration that is hidden somewhere in the solitude he is enjoying. At this point he is disturbed by a tiny, insignificant creature, a "creep," who knows him and recognizes him. He is so insignificant that he has no name, but he sees that he might become known as the "creep who has sat by Snufkin's camp-fire": perhaps Snufkin can invent a name for him? Snufkin is less than sociable, and the disturbance of his peace means that his incipient melody disappears entirely; however, he does provide the creature with a name-- Teety-woo--before wandering off toward the north. Now his conscience starts to trouble him, for he has been

67

unkind toward a creature who was obviously seeking contact, and he decides to go back and make amends. There is a new moon, and Snufkin uses his customary wish to wish that he might find Teety-woo. When he finally tracks him down, he finds that Teety-woo has undergone a transformation since receiving a name and an identity of his own; he is now too busy to be bothered with him. So Snufkin can withdraw into his solitude again; he lies down on a grassy bank, and his melody comes.

Like much of Tove Jansson's work, this story operates on two levels, but as was the case in <u>Moominland Midwinter</u>, it is the less immediately obvious of the two that is the important one. The plot is slender indeed, and the interest appears to be centered on character rather than action as such. However, the symbolical or allegorical content is the important feature, for Snufkin, who has previously been shown to write poems and songs, is here the artist wrestling with the problems of the artist--the need for solitude, the role of inspiration, the demands made on him, his responsibility to others, and his influence on others. In the wish he makes to the new moon, a further aspect of the artist's problem is hinted at: his usual wish is for a new melody or occasionally "a new direction," that is, some form of artistic inspiration. But in this case, his wish concerns his growing feeling of responsibility toward a fellow creature. It is only when he has come to terms with "human" demands that his inspiration returns to him. This consideration of the artist's problems comes at a time when Tove Jansson herself appears to be looking in a new direction, experimenting with new forms of expression. The fact that she clothes her artist in the guise of a musician does not hide the true meaning, and she is not the first writer to express the writer's problems through another medium of artistic creation. Indeed, considering that she is both a writer and a painter, it seems natural that in an effort to distance herself from the immediate problem, she should express it via a musician.

In view of the fact that Moomintroll is consistently depicted as Snufkin's closest friend, it is not surprising that Snufkin's innermost feelings should be reflected through his thoughts about Moomintroll. He thinks of him waiting for him and imagines him (obviously a more mature Moomintroll than earlier) saying how he understands that Snufkin needs to be on his own at times, an imagined remark that probably throws light both on Snufkin and on the growing Moomintroll and that later takes on a new significance when Moomintroll goes off to live on his own in <u>Moominpappa at Sea</u>. Moomintroll's own stirrings are then reflected in Snufkin's sense of his "hopeless longing." Later, however, when Teety-woo says that Moomintroll will be waiting for Snufkin--that is, a situation conforming to what he himself has been imagining--Snufkin replies that he will go back to Moomintroll when he feels like it and not before. Taken together, these two examples of opposite reactions to the same situation appear to indicate the innate tension in Snufkin the artist, the tension between the longing for company and the need for solitude, the knowledge that other people can make claims on him and the desire to avoid them.

A similar inner conflict is hinted at in his meeting with the originally nameless Teety-woo, when it becomes obvious that Snufkin is the fêted celebrity known by all; he wants to be left alone and is aware that the demands made on him because of his position can destroy his creative ability. During his meeting with this creature, whose pathetic aspect is reminiscent of that of some of the visitors in <u>Moominland Midwinter</u>, his tune disappears along with his peace of mind, and it only returns when that peace of mind is restored by his coming to terms with the demands made on him. Again the conflict is sensed when Teety-woo asks Snufkin whether it is not wonderful to have someone who is missing you and is waiting for you, words that indicate loneliness on the part of the creature who so far has been so insignificant that he has no name and that are used at the same time to underline Snufkin's own desire for solitude. The two levels, thus, are indicated through one remark. And Snufkin confirms the disturbing effect on him of having to talk about himself:

> "Can't they understand that I'll talk it all to pieces if I have to tell about it. Then it's gone, and when I try to remember what it really was like, I remember only my own story." (16) [14]

"The Spring Tune" is a concentrated, poetical short story in which Tove Jansson succinctly treats a theme often encountered in creative writers. It hints at her own position as a creative writer in great public demand, but it also points to the added problem of the direction her work was to take in the future.

This problem is scarcely present in "A Tale of Horror," which reverts to the question of reality. Only in this case it is reality in the mind, and the story is a brief exploration of a child's ability to convince itself of something it knows to be false. In its way, the story begins to explore the borderline between any kind of objective reality and what a vivid imagination suggests might be true. A small whomper is playing with his even smaller brother and frightens him with his fantasies of red Indians and the prospect of death on the prairie. When the smaller brother starts crying in fear, the elder one leaves him, goes home over some marshy ground, and makes up a story that the younger brother has been swallowed up by a snake. He ends by believing it himself and later convinces his parents. When the truth is discovered, he is accused of making things up, but he is not quite sure whether he has done so or not. Deprived by an unimaginative father of his supper, he goes off, succeeds in frightening himself once more, and takes refuge in a mymble's house where, in his turn, he is terrified by a story of a deadly fungus which Little My tells him, though apparently without believing it herself.

This is certainly a story <u>about</u> children, but it is also a serious study of the interplay of reality and imagination and the inability of many people to distinguish between them. Related to the later study of a sick mind in "Locomotive," it is a step forward in the presentation of reality as being relative.

It also indicates the rigidity and perhaps insufficiency of the adult concept of reality: "They simply drew a line straight through all things and declared that on one side of it everything was believable and useful, and on the other side everything was simply thought up and useless" (29) [27]. This neat, adult division between the real and the unreal is reminiscent of the hemulens in the early work. In fact, at this stage, it becomes clear that the hemulens are intended to represent a specific type of middle-class, unimaginative respectability, a fact underlined by Snufkin's remark to himself in "The Spring Tune" to the effect that he has heard a rumor that some hemulens actually change for dinner, though he cannot imagine that this can be true.

Hemulens play an indirect part in the next story, "The Fillyjonk Who Believed in Disasters," as it is a hemulen house in which the fillyjonk lives, and it is a hemulen who has persuaded her that the house was once inhabited by her grandmother.

In itself the story is simple. The fillyjonk lives in a comfortless house on a desolate shore and fears that the calm weather presages a disaster. She is expecting a visit from Gaffsie, whose standards of etiquette she does her best to meet, but she fails miserably and she knows it. Gaffsie makes polite conversation: this is her level, and she is incapable of understanding the obsessive fillyjonk when she admits her overpowering sense of impending disaster, a feeling she obviously has all the time. Gaffsie leaves, and rings soon afterwards to hear whether the fillyjonk often has these feelings.

A storm comes on, growing in intensity until it blows off the chimney and breaks a window. The terrified fillyjonk, who has tried to hide in the larder and has made a vain attempt to telephone to Gaffsie, leaves the house and goes out into the storm, where she immediately feels less insecure. The dawn comes and with it an enormous waterspout which carries off her house. All she has left is a carpet which she was washing in the sea at the beginning of the story. She rinses it in the sea again; then she actually floats on it for a time and is then submerged:

> She dived headlong in a large green swell, she sat on her carpet and surfed on sizzling white foam, she dived again, down and down.
> One swell after the other came rolling over her, transparently green, and then the fillyjonk came to the surface again, for a breath, to look at the sun, spluttering and laughing and shouting and dancing with her carpet in the surf.
> Never in her life had she had such fun. (60) [58]

The neurosis from which she had obviously been suffering is gone; she has been healed by the storm on the one hand and the symbolical cleansing in the sea on the other. When Gaffsie comes to find her, the fillyjonk is completely relaxed and able to repeat Gaffsie's own indifferent comments from the preceding day, after which she sits and laughs until the tears run from her eyes.

The question has already been raised of the extent to which some of the novels and stories must be taken at their face value and the extent to which they have to be understood on a symbolical level. That question poses itself here even more significantly. Is the reader really to believe in the storm that results in the destruction and final disappearance of the fillyjonk's house, or is the drama to be seen as taking place in the fillyjonk's mind? The tempestuous events in nature are so closely and carefully linked to the tempestuous events taking place in the fillyjonk's mind that it is virtually impossible to separate the two, while the disappearance of the house in the whirlwind relieves her of the material cause of her oppression and leaves her in a balanced mental state. Her sense of insecurity when originally faced with Gaffsie has disappeared. This creature, who has obviously suffered from a sense of insufficiency and an obsessive need to cope with a situation that is beyond her, has emerged from an isolation that her very insufficiency imposed upon her.

The story of the fillyjonk who believed in disasters is far beyond the reach of children, and it represents yet another step in the progression from the children's book to adult writing, as well as being a sign of Tove Jansson's growing preoccupation with the problems of loneliness, obsession, and the inability to communicate with others. In this story of mental derangement, fear, and final resolution, all that is needed to remove all traces of the children's book is to change the names of the characters and to remove the occasional indication that they are not ordinary human beings. Even the illustrations indicate this development; the fillyjonk and Gaffsie have shapes now that are more and more recognizably human.

Yet the transition is not complete, and the next story, "The Last Dragon in the World," is back more or less on the child's level of comprehension. Moomintroll finds a tiny dragon which he takes into his room in a tin. When it is freed and has demonstrated that it is indeed a dragon--by breathing tiny flames--it turns its attention to Snufkin, from whom it refuses to be separated. Moomintroll is upset at this, and in order to avoid causing him deep disappointment, Snufkin bribes a hemulen to carry off the dragon and not release it until it is unlikely to find its way back. If the story is to be given a deeper significance, it must be that Snufkin is willing to make sacrifices for his young friend who might be growing up but has not yet made it. Snufkin's indolence is accompanied by great tenderness and understanding.

The outsider, the lonely creature who is not understood, is again the center of "The Hemulen Who Loved Silence." This particular hemulen is different from his relatives who, it is said, are big, noisy, backslapping creatures who scare everyone even though they mean well. They mean well with this hemulen, though they have never understood him. They cannot conceive of anyone who does not want to make noise and enjoy himself; it is beyond their understanding that a hemulen, or anyone else for that matter, should want peace and quiet. When the hemulen finally convinces them that he wants to retire and live a quiet life so that he can build the doll's house of his dream (a forerunner of the one in The Doll's House?), they laugh so much that his dream is spoiled. But they give him an old unused park to build his house in, and there at first he enjoys the silence and resents being disturbed by the little whomper whose meekness can be compared to that of the nameless creature in "The Spring Tune." He comes with food for the hemulen, and he and others persuade him that instead of building a useless house for his own private amusement, he should reconstruct something like the fairground he used to work in before floods destroyed it. It emerges that this hemulen has been kind to the children, has let them into the fairground without tickets, and in general has made himself loved by them. Grudgingly he starts to reconstruct the fairground, but it is to be a quiet place in which people can enjoy themselves without noise. In the end, he achieves his objective, to the bewilderment of his uncle who peers in through the gateway and then goes off with the barrel organ he had brought to provide music for the fairground.

It is a story related to "The Spring Tune," a tale of a desire for solitude in conflict with the need to do something for others. The hemulen is akin to the artist, though unlike Snufkin he is not as obviously artistic. However, his desire to construct the most beautiful doll's house in the world does perhaps indicate a certain artistic streak, though his intention to make its rooms "serious, empty and silent" is a hint of how far removed he is from the world around him. His determination to build it becomes almost an obsession, though the laughter of the other hemulens prevents this from happening. More lightweight than the earlier stories dealing with the artist's problems and obsession, this nevertheless touches on easily recognizable themes.

The same is true of the title story, "The Invisible Child," in which the transformation theme implicit in a number of the earlier stories is also apparent. Snufkin underwent a change that removed his inner tension; the fillyjonk emerged from some kind of oppressive neurosis; the hemulen found a peace he had longed for but not known before. Now Ninny, the invisible child, also undergoes a change, which is signified by her becoming visible again. Too-ticky arrives at the Moomin house with Ninny who has become invisible because of the harsh treatment meted out to her by a non-understanding aunt. She is presented to the Moomin family: "'Now, here's your new family. They're a bit silly at times but rather decent, largely speaking'" (107) [105]. It is left to them to bring her back to her normal state. Mamma finds a recipe for a cure which she adds to Ninny's coffee, but her gradual re-emergence is obviously principally due to the kindness and understanding which the family as a whole, but especially Mamma, show her. Finally only her face remains invisible, and nothing the family can do will bring it back, until Ninny, who has never seen the sea before, sees Pappa approaching Mamma, apparently with the intention of throwing her in. Ninny rushes at him and bites him in fury--and thereby regains her face. She has needed gentleness and understanding in order to thrive, and then she has needed an opportunity to assert her true personality. The oppressed child, suffering from a condition that is parallel to the fillyjonk's neurosis, has now emerged, and like the fillyjonk she celebrates her emergence by laughing almost uncontrollably--as is clearly shown in the vignette at the end of the story.

Too-ticky makes her second appearance in "The Invisible Child," but in a lesser role than that in <u>Moominland Midwinter</u>. In both she is concerned with invisible creatures—one remembers the invisible shrews in <u>Moominland Midwinter</u>—and with enabling someone to develop into what he or she really is. Both Moomintroll and Ninny are enabled to find themselves; in both cases Too-ticky finds the means of achieving what she wants, though the part she herself plays is that of providing the means rather than directly governing the process.

It is not clear whether "The Secret of the Hattifatteners" actually deals with the resolution of a neurosis or a fixed idea, or whether it can be seen as the way in which Pappa finds himself. In any event, it represents the ending of a profound longing which Pappa has apparently had since being very young when, according to <u>The Exploits of Moominpappa</u>, he was first attracted to the hattifatteners. Now that the story of his dissolute life with them is to be told, it seems that it was not so dissolute as all that; perhaps it was even a disappointment to Pappa.

Pappa suddenly disappears without a trace. However, Mamma is not worried: he has obviously done this sort of thing before, and he has always come back. And so he does this time, too. Perhaps Mamma has more insight into his innermost nature than he himself has. He follows an urge which he only partly understands, going off to a desolate stretch of coast people seldom visit, where there are no roads and where he has once seen the hattifatteners' boats. It appears that he is expected, for he has not been there long when a boat containing three hattifatteners appears. By means of signs, the hattifatteners indicate to Pappa that he is to go with them, which he does. They call at a small island where they go ashore and find a roll of birchbark—Pappa follows them but retires hastily to the boat when he comes across a host of tiny spiders. They follow him but retreat when the hattifatteners return. The company sails on, visiting various islands and collecting and depositing birchbark rolls, until they reach a larger, mysterious island where they are joined by others. Pappa greets them all and is greeted in turn by each of them; he has for some time felt all desires leaving him and sensed that perhaps he was becoming more like a hattifattener himself. A great thunderstorm comes on, obviously connected with the hattifatteners, who are filled with electric charges, and Pappa is bowled over by it. This brings him to himself: he rushes down to the boats, takes one, and sets sail for his comfortable life at home.

As in the case of the fillyjonk who believed in catastrophes, it is possible to see this either as a "real" story or as something taking place in the mind, possibly even as a dream. There are various allusions to dreams, and the nightmare effect of the spiders could be explained by this. However, whether it is dream or reality, it is obviously again a story of a mental breakthrough of some kind. The hattifatteners are creatures who instill fear; it is not considered good form to talk about them. They obviously constitute an irresistible attraction to Pappa, the opposite of the comfortable, respectable, and uneventful life he lives with his family in Moomin Valley. It is clear that he goes off to find himself--as the other creatures in these stories have found themselves--but that he finally discovers that he <u>is</u> himself, living his respectable life on the veranda at home, a life the hattifatteners have expressly been said to threaten. They have been spoken of disparagingly by the hemulens, who themselves are the epitome of the narrow and unimaginative middle class, and Pappa has been attracted by something completely different from his usual surroundings and way of life, the base urges that have hitherto been suppressed in his life. What happens is that he finds himself losing the purpose in his life, drifting into an existence in which he surrenders his being and his desires: "Never in his life had Moominpappa felt so at ease and pleased with everything" (125) [123]. "He was quite free, but he just didn't seem to have any likings any more" (135) [133]. He is like the hero in a science fiction novel who is drained of his innermost being; he feels himself becoming more and more like a hattifattener until he experiences the thunderstorm which has the same dramatic, even traumatic effect upon him as his attempt to push Mamma into the sea has on Ninny: he suddenly emerges as himself and goes home. The next time his yearning to change his life comes over him, he takes his family with him in <u>Moominpappa at Sea</u>, and again the indication at the end of <u>Moominvalley in November</u> is that they once more return to the peace and relative tranquility of Moomin Valley.

It is again a sudden event that in "Cedric" leads someone to find her real self--and that to some extent has an influence on Sniff, the most thoroughly selfish of all Tove Jansson's creations. Attracted by Moomintroll's words to the effect that you receive back tenfold anything you give away, Sniff has given away his favorite possession, Cedric, a toy dog with topaz eyes. He does not receive ten in return and is heartbroken. At this, Snufkin relates a story about an aunt who lived a selfish life and was generally unloved and unhappy. She swallowed a bone, and it was thought that this would result in her death. She had never really lived, never achieved her life's ambitions, but as she lay in bed awaiting death, she decided to give away all her possessions to her many relatives. When she had emptied her house of everything except her four-poster bed, the family gathered around her, and she laughed so happily (like the fillyjonk and Ninny) that she coughed up the bone. Now, a happy woman, she sold her bed, which was made of gold, and was able to fulfill most of her ambitions. Sniff only partly understands the story, but when he finds his Cedric--minus the topaz eyes--he takes it back and loves it for its own sake and not for its value.

This very short story is completely in harmony with the rest of the book; it is a tale of the need for consideration and respect for others, the need to find and fulfill oneself. And as in the other stories, the aunt's insight into her own nature results from a sudden and radical event.

Consideration for and kindness to others is fundamental to the last of the stories in the collection, "The Fir Tree." Many authors have tried to give a new meaning to the celebration of Christmas, and in this beautiful story, Tove Jansson joins them.

A hemulen, typically enough preoccupied with the practical aspects of Christmas preparations, awakens the Moomin family and tells them that Christmas is coming. They have no idea what he means, but they go out into the snow, which Pappa sees for the first time and has to have explained to him by Moomintroll. There they see people hurrying about buying Christmas trees and Christmas presents. They sense an approaching catastrophe, but they do as Gaffsie says and find a Christmas tree. They are told to "dress" it, to decorate it, but they still have no idea what to do. Here the tiniest, humblest creatures come out again and suggest how it should be decorated. And presents, they are told, should be left "for Christmas," whatever

Christmas is. This, too, is done, and candles are lit, and the tiny creatures who until now have seen Christmas celebrated only from a distance, are able for the first time to experience it for themselves. All the presents are given to them. It is a real Christmas for them, in its way contrasting with the bustle of Christmas associated with Gaffsie and the hemulens. With the peace comes drowsiness to the Moomin family, and they retire to finish off their hibernation.

The title, "The Fir Tree," reminds one of Hans Christian Andersen, but the image, though in its glory and splendor reminiscent of the Andersen story, has a different implication in that somehow the true spirit of Christmas is felt in this story, and it is associated with the Moomin family, enriching their experience even though they do not understand what it is about. In the novel <u>Moominland Midwinter</u>, the experience of winter changes Moomintroll. In this case, a winter experience enriches the lives of the family. They undergo a change, even if it is almost imperceptible, partly by conforming to a reality that is beyond their comprehension, whereby this final story is seen to fit the pattern of the book as a whole.

## Chapter Nine
## *Moominpappa at Sea*

<u>Moominpappa at Sea</u> can be seen as the last of the Moomin novels proper, in that it is the last in which the family takes a direct part. <u>Moominland in November</u> takes place in Moomin Valley, even in the Moomin house, but nothing is seen of the family itself. In not bringing the family back to the tranquility of the home they leave at the beginning of the novel, Tove Jansson has broken with her traditional pattern; however, a return might possibly be seen on a different level, in the reunification of the family which is otherwise split and divided. At the end, the family is changed but united once more, and their customary devotion to each other and their sense of closeness have re-emerged and reasserted themselves. At the same time, they have taken stock of certain aspects of reality that have been in danger of being overlooked, and they have adjusted to a new view of them. It is possible to talk of the establishment of an entirely new kind of harmony in the family, one based on respect and acceptance rather than convention.

### A Family Divided and Reunited

As the story begins, Pappa feels unwanted and useless. Everyone else is busy, but he is superfluous. Conscious of how the summer heat has dried up the vegetation, he warns the others of the danger of fire, but when Moomintroll finds a tiny fire while Pappa is asleep, he tells Mamma who puts it out before waking Pappa up. This is a further indication to him that he is superfluous, but he cannot really accustom himself to the idea that the other members of the family can act without him. In his pique, Pappa goes out into the garden where he is able to watch the family in a magic sphere, feeling there that they are small enough for him to hold in his hand. In better spirits he goes home, only to discover that Mamma has found the evening dark enough to light the lamp for the first time--

without asking him. The Groke, now described as a
nuisance rather than a danger, is also attracted by the
light and warmth of the lamp, and from the frozen patch
she leaves behind her, Moomintroll realizes that she
has been there and becomes interested in her. He goes
out early the following morning and finds Pappa in the
woodshed making a model lighthouse. This sight of
Pappa's make-believe world leads to the revelation that
he dreams of an island with a lighthouse on it and is
so convinced of its existence that he is prepared to
sail away with his family to find it.

Led by Pappa's instinct, and followed at a distance
by the Groke, they find the island. But the lighthouse, far bigger than they had expected, is in darkness, and at first there is no sign of a key. They
finally gain access and establish themselves, though it
is a place lacking all traces of comfort, with only
bare, whitewashed walls. This is the island Pappa has
dreamed of, and Pappa now feels that he is in command:
he will be the one to see to everyone's needs here, and
everything must be left to him. He tells Mamma to ask
him if there is anything she does not understand, and
when he finds the deep pool in the middle of the
island, he immediately takes possession of it and says
that it is only for fathers. Mamma accepts all this,
though the fact that on the first night she sleeps without her handbag, the symbol of her dignity in the home,
indicates that she is not herself. Meanwhile, she sets
about seeing to the family's requirements as usual, and
imagines a kitchen garden and a flower garden. However, Pappa's preoccupation with trying to understand
his island and Mamma's preoccupation with her attempt
to create congenial surroundings lead them in different
directions.

Moomintroll goes off in his own direction, too,
exploring the island and finding a glade that is attractive, but is full of ants. He goes to ask his father
for advice on how to deal with them, but Pappa is too
busy constructing a breakwater to listen to him.
Again, the contact between two members of the family
has broken down. Moomintroll embarks on establishing
contact with entirely different beings--the Groke on
the one hand calls on his sense of responsibility and
on the other, the sea horses appeal to his incipient
erotic instincts--and at the same time he feels attracted to the romantic solitude of his glade, rather in
the same way as Snufkin was torn between solitude and

commitment in "The Spring Tune." He finds a horseshoe belonging to one of the sea horses, whom he tries to find. He discovers two, whose charms are not entirely unlike those of the vain Snork Maiden, and he is fascinated by these obviously feminine creatures. However, they laugh at him, teasing him for his shape and for what they see as his childishness in giving the horseshoe to his mother. So he asks for it back, and Mamma, true to her nature, gives it without asking why. However, even this does not gain him the favors of the flirtatious sea horses.

Moomintroll's interest in the Groke is of a different kind. He is at first fascinated by her alien nature, but his approach to her gradually becomes more positive, and he embarks upon an attempt to thaw her out. When he is most infatuated with the sea horses, he tends to neglect the Groke, but after they disappoint him, he devotes more and more attention to her and finally succeeds in gaining her confidence and making her dance and sing.

While this has been going on, Pappa has been busy reflecting on the nature of the island, especially trying to explain the deep pool in the middle of it; he has also been trying to provide for the material needs of the family. His original attempt at netting fish is a failure, as is his attempt to build a breakwater, but he then sets about angling with which he becomes obsessed. He provides far too many fish for the family needs and is offended when they try to stop him. He is engrossed in his new occupations and has little contact with the rest of the family.

Mamma is also almost oblivious of the turn things have taken, and she only responds absentmindedly when Moomintroll announces that he wants to go to live in his glade for a time. Neither she nor Pappa really understands what is happening to him, but they make no attempt to interfere. Their silence, however, results from their personal preoccupations rather than from respect for what he is doing. Meanwhile, Mamma does begin to sense the dissolution of the family and makes one effort to bring them together by suggesting a Sunday outing:

> "There's danger in the air," Moominmamma shouted back. "If we don't go for a picnic this very instant, <u>anything</u> might happen to us!" (140) [119]

Within limits the outing is a success: it is as though something falls into place again, and they begin to talk to each other in a normal way, "not about the sea, not about the island and not about Moomin Valley," that is, not about the things by which they are each obsessed in one way or another. To Mamma, Moomin Valley is still home, and she longs to go back there. She now tries to re-create it on the island by painting familiar trees and flowers on the whitewashed walls. So intense is her longing to return that she actually moves into the garden she has painted and disappears to the family for a time. Realizing what she is doing, she now paints several pictures of herself on the walls so that she can withdraw into the new garden she has created for herself without her absence being noticed. Nevertheless, the success of the Sunday outing is now betokened by her interest in what Moomintroll is doing, and she goes with him one night to see his glade.

Pappa is convinced of the existence of some special relationship between the sea and himself, and he spends much of his time trying to understand the sea and discover the link between it and the deep pool, where the level of the water rises and falls with no apparent cause. In so doing, of course, he is moving into the sphere of pointless speculation and neglecting his duty to the realities by which he is surrounded.

The Groke also disturbs the normal life on the island, and one morning, Moomintroll awakens to find that the undergrowth has moved, fleeing from the Groke toward the lighthouse.

Meanwhile, there is another person on the island, a fisherman whom the family first encounters on the voyage. He avoids them and lives a secluded life; he is unwilling to enter into any contact or conversation, and Pappa finds him the most difficult person to make contact with he has ever known. He asks him what has happened to the lighthouse keeper, but the fisherman says he does not know. His loneliness is made very obvious, as is that of the mysterious lighthouse keeper, whose few verses expressing a longing for human contact come to light.

During a great storm the fisherman's house is washed away, and its occupant almost suffers the same fate. Pappa and Moomintroll work together to rescue him, Moomintroll now for the first time working with Pappa as an equal and Pappa actually doing something useful.

The fisherman is still unwilling to go to the lighthouse with them, but they discover that the following day is his birthday, and they arrange a party in his honor. After a lot of persuasion they manage to coax him inside, when it gradually emerges that he <u>is</u> the lighthouse keeper. The keeper has returned, the trauma of loneliness has been broken, and he now fulfills his proper function by going to the top of the tower and lighting the lamp that Pappa has been unable to get working. Pappa, for his part, has come to terms with the sea in the sense that he accepts it without trying any longer to understand it:

> All Moominpappa's thoughts and speculations vanished. He felt completely alive from the tips of his ears to the tip of his tail. (208) [176]

He has surrendered himself to everyday reality instead of building an artificial world which was only a real world to himself. He has moreover accepted Moomintroll's growing up. As for Mamma, she has invited the fisherman "home" for the first time (180) [152] instead of talking of going back to the lighthouse; <u>her</u> acceptance of the new reality is represented by her suddenly no longer being able to enter her painted garden, because she is no longer homesick. Moomintroll has been forced to accept reality in losing the sea horses, but he has channeled his energies in a more responsible direction by making contact with the Groke.

Thus, the novel ends with all the characters accepting their surroundings instead of obsessively trying to create a romanticized reality for themselves. The only person in the book not to undergo a change is Little My, who throughout has been the voice of unadorned down-to-earth reality, bringing back all the members of the family from their frequent flights of fancy. It has throughout been her task to remove illusions, check pretensions, and blurt out the unadorned truth. She is completely ruthless in her actions, completely devoid of the sentimentality and emotionalism that is part of the Moomin makeup. She acts provocatively in order to face people with reality, as when she takes up Moomintroll's hint that he would like the ants removed from his glade: she kills them all with paraffin and dismisses his ensuing moral protest with the scorn it deserves; through this action she shows him that he cannot avoid accepting the responsibility for a situation he has been instrumental in creating, even if his role was a passive one.

Little My is, of course, different from the other characters, existing perhaps mainly for her function. Her language is different, sharper, less subjective than that of the Moomintrolls, and she is, of course, not really one of them, but an adopted daughter. Her standards of behavior are different from their middle-class respectability, and she mercilessly points to the difference between what they say and do and what they really mean on more than one occasion.

### Pappa

The title of the novel firmly places Pappa at the center, though in this connection it should be noted that the Swedish title of "Pappa and the Sea" lacks the overtones of the English "Moominpappa at Sea," but lays greater emphasis on the relationship between Pappa and the sea.

In the earlier Moomin books, Pappa has played an important but not a dominant role. He has been second in the hierarchy, coming after Mamma, except in the memoirs, which of course are written by himself and perhaps show a tendency to overcompensate. That the quiet and self-effacing Pappa has other sides to his nature, which appear to have been suppressed either by his hemulen upbringing or by Mamma's gentle but firm rule, has been clear from his early references to his dissolute life with the hattifatteners and from his adventure with them in the short story "The Secret of the Hattifatteners." Seen within the framework of the Moomin stories as a whole, Pappa has occasionally tried to play a different part, but has always ultimately returned to the fold. As Moomintroll grows up and becomes more independent, Pappa's position is further undermined, and his patriarchal dream is no longer even remotely realizable.

This is the situation at the beginning of Moominpappa at Sea. Pappa is no more superfluous than he was before, but he feels himself to be so, and his obsessive concern with the possibility of a fire and his study of "the way fire burns" (9) [11] indicate at a very early stage that he is impractical and unrealistic as well as overly concerned with his own importance as the pater familias. He feels humiliated when Mamma puts out the tiny fire of her own accord, easily and without calling on him for help. Things become even worse when he finds that Mamma has lit the lamp without asking his permission: "In some families it's the father who decides when to light the lamp" is his complaint (15) [15]. The following morning he retreats to his toy lighthouse, his own world, a fantasy world where he seeks refuge--a situation that was to be fundamental in many of the stories in The Doll's House thirteen years later.

However, what was to become the "doll's house" motif takes a peculiar twist in this novel, in that Pappa actually seeks to turn his dream world into reality by taking his family with him to "his" island where, he imagines, he will be in complete control. Pappa has convinced himself that the island exists, although he has never actually been there, and it seems that he is guided there by some profound and primitive Moomin instinct:

> "Just a moment, I must get my bearings," said Moominpappa. He spread out the map on the sand and stared at the island, all by itself right out in the open sea. He was very serious. He sniffed in the wind for a while and tried to get his sense of direction, something he hadn't had to use for a long time. "Our ancestors never needed to worry about finding the right course, it came to them naturally of its own accord. It's a pity that the instinct gets weaker if you don't use it." (25) [23]

In following this primitive instinct, Pappa seems again to be seeking a situation that no longer really exists. The island might be there, but it is different from what he has expected, and the family structure he is hoping to build there is to prove impossible. The first sign that he is not going to be able to achieve his objective is the disappearance of the key. Until that is found Pappa is unable to act, and even when he does find it--by instinct or luck--on the former keeper's "lonely spot" and takes his family into the lighthouse, he is not able to turn on the light. In his own eyes he is now the lighthouse keeper, and in that role he hopes to achieve a new structure. He fails. His frustration is then reflected in a nightmare in which he dreams of trying and failing to get to the top of the lighthouse and light the lamp. After acknowledging the impossibility of realizing his aspirations, he is given comfort in the form of a sandwich that Mamma makes for him.

It is at this stage that Pappa begins unconsciously to withdraw from the family. He sets about building his breakwater--an act that interferes with the natural relationship between the sea and the island; the sea smashes it to pieces. The attempt is, then, yet another failure. Pappa is so engrossed in his task that he loses contact with his family, showing little interest in or understanding of what they are doing. His fishing expedition with the nets is again an act of defiance toward the sea, and the sea once more humiliates him by filling the net with seaweed. He comments that everything in the outlying islands is a battle with the sea--but it is in fact a battle he has lost. He is again set at a distance from the family when Mamma and Moomintroll spend two days clearing the nets while he simply reflects and then makes a--not entirely successful--belt for Mamma, decorating it with rice at a time when food supplies are running low. In his desire to provide for his family, he now tries angling, and in striking contrast to the lonely fisherman, he catches all the perch he wants and more besides. He now becomes obsessed with fishing, so that Mamma is almost in despair at the number of fish he brings. However, she understands the truth behind Pappa's apparent success--it is the sea that is being "nasty" to him, teasing him. Pappa is not fortunate: on the contrary, it is his misfortune that he becomes so taken up with his task that he is blind to everything else, and Mamma begins to feel that things were better when the family was going hungry.

Pappa now goes on to "reflect" on the pool, trying to understand its strange behavior and suspecting the sea is responsible for it. He again becomes dominated by his interest, as indicated in a brief exchange between him and Mamma. It is reminiscent of one between him and Moomintroll, when Moomintroll wants to talk about sea horses but his father is interested only in building his breakwater. This time Mamma has found some shells for which she has been searching, and she comes to show them to Pappa. He is not interested.

Her cry of "Look at these shells" is met with "This lake is very interesting." Contact between the two has ceased, and Mamma fails to elicit any kind of response. Pappa continues trying to "understand," but he fails, just as he fails to understand why the undergrowth on the island is moving. Yet he will not admit his failure: "It was awful to be forced to say, 'I don't know.' He was fed up with not understanding anything" (169) [143]. Pappa's urge to understand everything is again referred to in a discussion with Moomintroll, in which Pappa admits that he understands less than ever, but is still determined to discover the hidden laws of the sea: "I must [understand it] if I'm going to learn to like it. I shall never be happy on this island until I've learned to like the sea" (171) [145]. In this important conversation, Pappa then goes on to stumble on a hidden truth: "There's no rhyme or reason in it. And if there is, it's more than I can understand." Moomintroll, who feels flattered because for the first time Pappa is talking to him as a grown-up, significantly but somewhat ambiguously comments that he is sure that his father would understand it if there were one. The climax is approaching.

The dénouement comes when the sea washes away the fisherman's house, and Pappa and Moomintroll work together to effect a rescue. There is now no question of understanding or reflecting, but of acting, and Moomintroll is again treated as an adult, acting in perfect unity with Pappa, who can even communicate with him without speaking--as has happened between Moomintroll and Snufkin. It is this experience of a direct confrontation with the sea instead of a useless attempt to reflect on it and understand it in the abstract that breaks the spell, and Pappa is transformed. He has come to respect the sea and view it in the right and natural perspective--and the sea responds by washing up the planks they need to proceed with their building and to establish themselves on the island. Significantly the whole family takes part in grasping the planks as they come in. The island is now Pappa's island, but on the right conditions, and after the birthday party for the fisherman, the lighthouse is lit not by Pappa, who has given up his reflections and pretensions and has decided to live instead, but by the fisherman, to whom the task properly belongs.

## Mamma

Parallel with Pappa's progression from dream and obsession to reality goes a similar transformation on the part of Mamma. In her case, it is a question of adapting to new surroundings and, perhaps, adopting a new role. As with Pappa, her point of departure is the pattern of family life with which the reader is well acquainted. She is the center of the family in the house in Moomin Valley; in this role she is able not only to look after the housekeeping but also to pacify Pappa when he is in a difficult mood, occasionally with a touch of irony in her "Yes dear." She certainly says that Pappa knows best, but she also appears to agree with Little My's more skeptical view on this point.

However, Mamma's role is very closely tied to Moomin Valley. The way in which she tells Moomintroll that they are to go and live on Pappa's island shows no trace of enthusiasm; rather she seems resigned. Because she is taken out of her accustomed surroundings, for a time she loses her customary role. Even in the boat on the way to the island, she adopts a passive role and decides to sleep. On arriving she has lost her authority, and the interplay between her and Pappa is both tragicomical and significant:

> She shook herself, as though to break the silence, and began to poke about among her baskets, trying to get the box of earth with her roses over the side of the boat.
> "Now, take it easy," said Moominpappa nervously. "I'll look after all this. Everything must be properly organised from the beginning. The boat is always the most important thing. . . . You sit still and take it easy."
> Moominmamma sat down obediently, trying not to get in the way of the sail as it came down . . . while Moominpappa scrambled about the boat organising things. (33) [30]

It is not often one sees Mamma reduced to this. Nor is it often that she meekly accepts that she must do as Pappa says, as when immediately afterwards she creeps into the little tent he has made for her. Moomintroll watches her settle down and thinks how different things are--it is unusual for Mamma not to see to the family

*Moominpappa at Sea* 89

before going to bed herself. In addition, she has put down her handbag. Moomintroll sees this as a positive thing, the sign of a real change in their lives, not merely a short-lived adventure.

The following day, Mamma sets about re-creating the surroundings she knows from Moomin Valley, looking for shells, for soil, for the possibility of cultivating a garden. She dislikes the lighthouse, feels it (rightly) to be bare and uninviting. She accepts without question the horseshoe Moomintroll gives her, being too concerned with her own thoughts to wonder where it has come from. In one sense she is as self-centered as Pappa at this point, and the way in which she collects rotting seaweed "with the same deep warm colour as the soil back there at home" also shows her to be as estranged from reality and as obsessed as Pappa, even if she still does see to the family's basic needs. The major symbolical action she undertakes is to paint the garden on the whitewashed walls, a sequel to her distracted painting of flowers on some of the windows. The intensity of her longing for Moomin Valley is symbolized by her "disappearing" into the garden she has painted, an ability she retains until she overcomes her homesickness. After the episode in which the sea washes the planks ashore and the whole family joins in saving them, Mamma, like Pappa, has changed. Like him, she now accepts the island on its own terms, referring to the lighthouse as home, and no longer trying to re-create her lost Moomin Valley paradise. When Moomintroll asks her whether the apple seed she has planted has come up, she laughs at him--though she would not have done at the time she planted it--and she realizes on seeing the dead rose trees she has transplanted how foolish it was to try to plant them in a garden--there are hosts of them on the island. Perhaps a natural landscape is better than a garden. After coming to this conclusion, she goes indoors and savors the harmony now reigning in the family. When no one is watching her, she goes across to her painted garden and tries to enter it. She cannot.

### Moomintroll

Moomintroll also changes and emerges into a new reality. This novel continues the process already begun in Moominland Midwinter, when he began to adapt to new surroundings. Now he passes from childhood into adolescence. He is happy at this prospect, which for him means a change in his own status. He wants to be grown up now, and seeks understanding from his parents of the new urges of which he is beginning to be aware. He wants to be treated as a responsible being, and yet he does not always want to accept responsibility. His desire for solitude in his glade shows an affinity to the Snufkin of "The Spring Tune," though the urge to be alone can also be seen as a sign of puberty. After announcing that he intends to stay in the glade for a time, he lives his own secret life, symbolized by his nightly encounters with the Groke and the sea horses. They represent aspects of Moomintroll's developing character, and it is significant that his meetings with them, always on the shore, are usually juxtaposed. It can thus be taken that they represent two conflicting claims being made on him at the same time. He is, for a while, strongly attracted to the sea horses, and thus joins the ranks of those obsessed characters who figure so prominently in Tove Jansson's later work, but his concern with them is not of the profounder kind, and his defeat in this field is not a great humiliation to him. In fact, he is fundamentally more concerned with the Groke who at first appeals to his curiosity, but later also to his sense of responsibility. She is one of the creatures who cannot make contact with others but who earnestly desire to do so, and so, despite Mamma's somewhat uncharacteristic warnings not to bother with the Groke, Moomintroll goes to greater lengths to make contact with her. He is able to do so precisely because the family is in a state of dissolution, and the other members are too preoccupied to be bothered.

Parallel with this process goes the establishment of contact with the lighthouse keeper, whose loneliness has become such that he could no longer live in the lighthouse (1). It has been almost as difficult to get on terms with him as it has been with the Groke, though in this case Moomintroll has not been the only one interested in doing so. All members of the family, including Little My, have tried, which perhaps gives the mysterious fisherman a special significance. He is the person who attracts everyone's attention, and it is his rescue that unites the family again, partly in the actual attempt, partly in the party they organize for him on his birthday. In his loneliness, he is not unlike the creature without a name in "The Spring Tune," and like Teety-woo, he is brought to life and activity when he is accepted into a group of people and given an identity--which he could not have when living alone. Just as they are now liberated from their obsessions, he is liberated from his loneliness, and he can take over his normal function at the same time as the family can act as a unit again. The lighting of the lamp is the sign that everything is restored to its proper place.

At the same time the natural vegetation of the island, which had been retreating in fear toward the lighthouse, soon returns to its natural place. It was frightened of the changes taking place on the island, and now that things have resumed their natural balance, it can go back to where it belongs. The use of the moving vegetation to underline the tension and to point to the approaching climax is a highly effective feature of this novel.

At the end a new harmony has been established. The different members of the family have gone through traumas of various kinds, experiences that were necessary if they were to be reunited. Pappa has given up his unrealistic aspirations and accepted normality; Mamma has adapted to new surroundings and accepted that she cannot re-create things as they were; Moomintroll has been accepted as more than a child by both of them, and he himself has learned to accept the responsibilities accompanying adulthood. All this has taken place against a background of human loneliness and, perhaps in the case of the Groke, of old age. Nature has been left undisturbed, and a modus vivendi established with it by the newcomers to the island.

A political message could be seen in this novel. Or an ecological message. Or it could be seen in a general psychological light as examining the claims of realism on the imagination. Or it could be seen as urging human kindness and a sense of responsibility toward those in need--certainly a theme that comes more and more to the foreground in Tove Jansson's later work. Or it can be seen as a novel about obsessions and preoccupations and their relationship to the uncomplicated ordinary life the Moomintrolls represent. Thus, it is a novel that can be read in many different ways. At the same time, when seen in the context of

Tove Jansson's work as a whole, it represents clearly the author's growing interest in the less rational aspects of human nature, the way in which people create their own small worlds and cut themselves off from the real world around them.

## Chapter Ten
# *Moominvalley in November*

In <u>Moominland Midwinter</u> Tove Jansson experimented with a Moomin novel almost without Moomins. Moomintroll is the only member of the family to play any real part in the story, though the adopted Little My also has a role. In <u>Moominvalley in November</u>, the author takes a step further and writes a novel set in and around the Moomin house in Moomin Valley, in which the significance of the family is constantly underlined, but not a single member of the family is actually seen. The nearest we get to them is a glimpse of the lantern on their boat on the last page.

While it could certainly be argued that <u>Moominpappa at Sea</u> is scarcely a children's novel, it would be hard to maintain that <u>Moominvalley in November</u> is at all to the taste of children. The book shows those aspects of people's natures that are normally hidden, those parts of their personalities that are suppressed but may well determine their behavior; it also shows how a group of people change under one another's influence. Indeed, although the characters are still dressed up as hemulens and fillyjonks, it is difficult to see them as anything but clearly differentiated human beings. For some time in Tove Jansson's work the tendency to move from the typical to the individualized has been apparent, but now, in <u>Moominpappa at Sea</u> and <u>Moominvalley in November</u>, she is no longer content to deal with human types who can easily be disguised as animals or fairy-tale creatures. Instead, she becomes increasingly concerned with the peculiarities of human nature, which makes it difficult for her to disguise her characters as anything but human beings. Whether or not she tired of the Moomin family, it seems that this growing interest in certain more complex aspects of human nature must have played its part in persuading her in later books no longer to disguise her characters, but to present them as the people they are.

Nevertheless, <u>Moominvalley in November</u> draws on the world she has gradually created, and there are

frequent references to earlier events and the absent
family. However, now that the family has been transformed in <u>Moominpappa at Sea</u>, the time has come to
bring about a transformation in the remainder of the
principal characters, particularly those who have shown
an increasing tendency to neuroses. In this respect,
it is perhaps significant that there is no mention of
the Groke in this novel: she was also transformed in
<u>Moominpappa at Sea</u>.

**A Novel of Transformation**

<u>Moominvalley in November</u> begins with a series of
chapters in which the various characters are seen in
isolation, each of them for one reason or another finally deciding to seek the security or warmth or hospitality represented by the Moomin family. Snufkin leaves in
his usual autumn migration, but he cannot recapture the
melody that was forming in his head during the summer,
and later he has to return to Moomin Valley to find it.
As in "The Spring Tune" it will only come of its own
accord and in the right circumstances. Toft, the
whomper who lives hidden in the hemulen's unused boat,
lulls himself to sleep each evening by inventing a
story about the Moomin family and their home, and he
feels an urge to find the valley and the home to discover whether the dream world he has created is really as
he imagined it. The fillyjonk, obsessively house-proud
and filled with loathing for insects, almost falls to
her death when standing on the sloping roof of her
house in order to clean the windows. After a nightmare
experience sliding round the outside and looking for a
way back into her familiar world, she decides to put
the cleaning aside and visit the Moomin family. The
hemulen, who means well but cannot get on with people,
feels attracted to the house in Moomin Valley: he has
only vague memories of the actual family, but he remembers liking their hospitality on a former occasion. He
decides to repeat the experience. This motley collection of beings, one tender and looking for a mother,
one conscientiously but obsessively house-proud, one
sensitive and artistic, one thick-skinned and unable to
understand why he cannot get on with people, gradually
congregate in the Moomin house where they are joined by
a difficult hundred-year-old man, Grandpa Grumble, and
by Mymble, who is a somewhat gentler edition of her

sister, Little My. It is a gathering of individuals each of whom lives in his or her own world, with little contact with anything outside it. The novel tells how that contact is established.

On the surface, it is an uneventful story. The various characters arrive, are disappointed on finding no one at home, and settle down together to make the best of the situation. At first they all try to remain unchanged and true to themselves; each is self-centered in his or her own way, each dominated by the obsessions and passions that are part and parcel of his or her fundamental nature--and Tove Jansson makes it clear that whatever changes come over them, they remain themselves. However, they do become slightly modified versions of what they have been hitherto. They become tolerant and more realistic versions of themselves, having come to terms with their own peculiarities instead of trying to turn themselves into the Moomin family, which represents their ideals and which they at times seek to emulate. The fillyjonk is disgusted at the state of the house, but she is too overwhelmed by her traumatic experience when cleaning her own home to start doing anything about it. The hemulen wants to organize everyone but only succeeds in dominating Toft and irritating the fillyjonk. Toft is disappointed over not finding the ideal Mamma of his dreams, and he retires to read a book he has found, the contents of which form an allegory to the story itself. Grandpa Grumble, suspicious of all around him, makes himself difficult with all the others, convinced that they are having fun behind his back, but he is content when he finds a figure in a dusty mirror whom he thinks of as Moomintroll's "ancestor" and who treats him with courtesy and silence. Mymble, like her rather less gentle sister My, spends her time placing the others' feet firmly on the ground. Snufkin does his best to avoid too much contact with the others, but it is a hopeless task, and he has to resign himself to the situation. Of all these characters, the fillyjonk, the hemulen, and Toft are at first filled with the desire somehow to be absorbed into the idealized Moomin world of their imaginations.

Although there is no central character in the novel, it is true to say that the fillyjonk is the most dynamic throughout much of it, and it is she who undergoes the most radical change. She is a difficult person, as is early made plain in Snufkin's view of her and of fillyjonks in general:

> Snufkin had met many fillyjonks in his time and knew that they had to do things in their own way and according to their own silly rules. (10) [6]

But tolerant as he is, he gives them as wide a berth as possible. The fillyjonk is conscientious but afraid of other people; she shuts herself off from other beings, thereby creating for herself the basis of the neurosis of which she is cured in the course of the novel. One sign of her state of mind is her horror of anything resembling an insect: early in the novel she sees one and immediately throws it off the roof, a path she is soon nearly to take herself when the other aspect of her neurosis, her obsession with cleaning, forces her out onto the same roof. Meanwhile, her desire to do the right thing by taking a present for Mamma conflicts with her selfishness, and she changes one rather splendid present for a more modest one--to which she constantly draws the attention of the others throughout the story. During her desperate attempts to get back into the house, the everyday world she can see through the window but not reach, she has resolved to change, and when she does finally save herself, her world really has taken on a different aspect, though it is still cold and comfortless. She leaves to look for "people who talked and were pleasant and went in and out and filled the whole day so that there was no time for terrible thoughts" (24) [22].

This is what she expects of the Moomin family. She is to be disappointed, because the warmth exuded by them is something that only they can engender: without them the house is empty and, symbolically, cold, and the fillyjonk retires to her north-facing room and shivers in conditions reminiscent of those she has known before, because she cannot herself transform them. She is afraid, as is recognized by both Toft and Mymble, dominated at first by her selfishness together with her fear of insects and bacteria, a fear that makes her angry with the hemulen who in true hemulen fashion tries to tidy everything and therefore rakes up all the leaves he finds in the autumn garden:

> "You musn't touch old leaves! They're dangerous!

They're full of putrefaction!" She dashed to the front of the veranda with the blankets trailing behind her. "Bacteria!" she screamed. "Worms! Maggots! Creepy-crawlies! Don't touch them!" (54) [52]

She quarrels with him, too, when the guests cannot agree who should wash up after dinner, something that surely must be natural to the house-proud fillyjonk, but that perhaps reminds her of the cleaning of which she now goes in fear. When the hemulen suggests that she should do it, she refuses on the (reasonable) ground that the hemulen always wants to organize other people.

Her obsession with tidiness also has implications for her person. She carefully puts her hair in curlers at night, though in the realm of hair she comes a poor second to Mymble, whose beautiful hair is referred to on more than one occasion.

In her efforts to assert herself and take the place of Mamma, however, the fillyjonk decides to light a fire in the stove, whereby she almost destroys the "ancestor"--though the "ancestor's" existence may be doubted, as he is never seen. In seeking to light the fire, however, the fillyjonk is unwittingly about to do the opposite of what Mamma has wanted: in a letter that has been found and taken--but not read--by Uncle, Mamma has expressly asked that the stove should not be lit, as the "ancestor" is in it.

However, the fillyjonk does begin to show signs of changing. One evening when she goes out as usual to empty a bucket, a task that she normally dislikes intensely and completes as quickly as possible, she pauses and hears Snufkin playing his mouth organ:

> But tonight Fillyjonk stood on the steps and listened to the darkness. Snufkin was playing in his tent, a beautiful, vague tune. Fillyjonk wasn't musical, although neither she nor anyone else realised it. She listened breathlessly. She forgot all the awful things; tall and thin, she was silhouetted against the lighted kitchen, an easy prey to all the lurking dangers of the night. But nothing happened. When the melody was finished she gave a deep sigh, put down the bucket and went back into the house. (93) [93]

It is doubtful whether the suggestion that the fillyjonk is becoming musical is to be taken at face value. Snufkin's search for his melody is very much a symbolical act, and the melody comes to stand for the peace of mind he knows he will find in the valley. Nevertheless, the fillyjonk's pleasure at the music does seem to be a sign that she herself is changing and becoming more harmonious, a change that is further indicated by her whistling and later by her efforts to play the mouth organ that Snufkin leaves lying around. One of her last acts before leaving the house is to ask him what sort of a mouth organ it is, as she would like to buy one for herself.

It is Snufkin who finally persuades the fillyjonk to go into the kitchen and make it her own, a further step in her path toward inner harmony. She is able to make a dinner with the fish caught by Grandpa Grumble, and in this way she brings the guests together around her achievement. She has become someone who means something to others, and she is now able to refer to the disparate group as a "family." However, when she tries to go even further and produce a meal like those that Moominmamma makes, she fails. She is not and cannot become Mamma, but she is able to achieve a positive significance of her own, and this is and must be enough for her. The final breakthrough is symbolized by her decision to spring-clean the entire house: the trauma has gone, and now, as a new and better fillyjonk, she is able to undertake the tasks that are natural to her. Moreover, she is able to infect the others with her enthusiasm. At the end she goes off, not this time alone, but accompanied by Mymble.

Like the fillyjonk, the hemulen ends as a modified version of himself. While the fillyjonk has really seen herself as another Mamma, the hemulen aspires to be like Pappa, and indeed on one occasion he says outright that he feels they have much in common--although at the beginning of the book he only seems to have a very vague idea of what the family is like. In his self-centered desire to find comfort and to organize others, he remembers the house and talks as though he is a frequent guest there. His view of Pappa, however, becomes in fact an idealized view of himself. He is a comic figure, but like many comic figures not without his tragic features, for he is early shown to be dissatisfied with himself but unable to do anything about it:

> He tried being the hemulen that everybody liked, he tried being the hemulen that no one liked. But however he tried he remained a hemulen doing his best without anything really coming off. (28) [25]

One of the hemulen's problems is that he tries to convince others that he is not what he really is, oblivious of the fact that they have seen through him. His pretended passion for sailing is used to indicate this side of his nature: Toft actually lives in his boat and knows perfectly well that it has never been on the water, and Snufkin also realizes that the hemulen's claims to love sailing and camping are false. He finally puts the hemulen to the test by actually taking him out in a boat, ignoring his violent seasickness and leaving him to steer. This is the event that transforms the hemulen, and by the time they reach land his seasickness has left him; his desire to sail has also gone, and with it the need to boost his ego by pretending to like it. He has accepted himself in this respect, just as he has already tacitly accepted that he is not another Pappa when the house he is building in a tree for Pappa is a failure; it finally falls down, leaving him (and the reader) with the conviction that perhaps that is the best thing that could happen to it.

Hemulens are without imagination or sensitivity. The great contrast between the hemulen and Toft is indicated by the fact that whereas Toft has never been to Moomin Valley, he finds his way without difficulty, but the hemulen, who has been there before, gets hopelessly lost on the way. His lack of sensitivity is also shown immediately on his arrival by the noisy and ridiculous way in which he puts in his appearance outside the empty house. It emerges again when he decides to spend the night in Snufkin's tent, thereby spoiling the peace with which Snufkin has been preparing to surround himself; the following morning he is the cause of Snufkin's falling over a rake (a symbol of the hemulen's activities), again spoiling the peace. He is oblivious to all this and fails to notice that Snufkin does not share his noisy delight in the early morning. Yet the night has had its effect, and the change that gradually takes place in the hemulen can be traced at least to this juncture:

> When the Hemulen approached the house the morning was over. Now the day was beginning for the others, they didn't know anything about what he'd been given. Fillyjonk opened her window to air the room.
> "Good morning!" the Hemulen called. "I slept in the tent! I heard all the noises of the night!"
> "What noises?" Fillyjonk asked sourly, and secured the window catch.
> "The noises of the night," the Hemulen repeated. "I mean the noises that one can hear in the night." (71) [69]

There is, of course, a touch of humor in this, but the similarity between the superficial and insensitive hemulen's experience of sound in this instance and the potentially more sensitive fillyjonk's experience of music cannot be overlooked. Both start by the experience of sound in the night.

Nor can it be overlooked that the hemulen is the person who makes the otherwise placid Snufkin lose his temper, by preparing to put up a notice. Snufkin is ardently opposed to notices of any kind, and he becomes very angry at this affront, innocent as it is. Curiously, his burst of temper also has its mellowing effect on the hemulen, who now looks on Snufkin with greater respect and in a more realistic light.

When the hemulen finally leaves, soon after his sail with Snufkin, Toft asks him what he is going to do with the boat. Toft has a certain interest in this question, as the hemulen's boat has so far been his home. The hemulen says he will get rid of it to the right person, not, he says, in answer to Toft's question, to someone who <u>dreams</u> of sailing, but to someone who needs it. He does not need it any longer--his dream of sailing has gone--and he is now in a state of balance within himself, hemulen though he still is.

It is not without significance here that Toft puts his question in terms of a dream, for a dream is his big problem. In his loneliness in the hemulen's boat, he has made up his own story of the Moomin family, their house, and their valley. This dream has grown and grown, although just before leaving to see the valley for himself, Toft does find that each time he goes through the story the outline becomes blurred at an earlier and earlier stage. However, he has dreamed so thoroughly and accurately that he finds the valley without difficulty. Everything is as he had imagined—apart from the fact that the house is empty. The accuracy of his dream seems to indicate that Toft has some affinity with the family, in which Mamma is his ideal. That there is something special and powerful about the whomper's imagination seems to be beyond all doubt. Indeed, with the possible exception of Snufkin, he is the only one of the characters in this book to have an identifiable imagination. In his disappointment at not finding the family in their home, he retires and reads a scientific work telling of a nummulite that strays from its family and starts to shrink and change, as it needs the electricity to which it has been accustomed in order to grow and develop.

At this stage the whomper starts applying his imagination to the nummulite, with whom he obviously feels some affinity, being small and neglected himself. He feels that by thinking of the nummulite he will be able to increase its size and thus save it. He thinks and thinks, and his imaginings are helped by a thunderstorm in which he feels that the nummulite must be growing. It is. When he goes out to the part of the valley where his instincts tell him it must be, he is met not by a tiny creature but by a monstrous growl from which he flees in terror. During the dinner party organized by the fillyjonk, he senses that the Creature, as it is now called, must be outside the house. Whereas in the case of the dream of Moomin Valley Toft's imagination has proved to be close to the truth, here it is as though his fantasies have gone completely out of control. Snufkin is the only other character to notice what is going on, and he warns Toft. "You should be careful not to let things get too big," he says, with words that might well make the reader wonder whether the Moomin family itself has grown too big for its creator. There are certainly overtones in the presentation of the conflict between fantasy and reality that could indicate that Tove Jansson has become highly subjective in this book. The general movement from an imaginary reality to an objective reality indicated in the development of each individual character could well symbolize the movement from fantasy worlds to the real world that is at the same time taking place in her work. It is also closely connected with the question of what reality is and with the obsession theme; thus it has both psychological and philosophical overtones.

However, Toft's Creature grows to its greatest size at the same time as Toft tries to assert his presence in his new surroundings. When, at the dinner, each character is to make some kind of contribution to the evening's entertainment, Toft reads from his scientific book a passage on aggressiveness. He has already shown that peaceable as he is, he can lose his temper and become aggressive, whereby he has discovered a side to his nature, the existence of which he did not know before, but to which he has to resign himself. And as he reads his piece, the Creature is itself outside, growing bigger and more threatening. There is an obvious connection between Toft's aggressiveness and that of the Creature he has created, as though it is a tangible representative of the hidden side of his nature. It is at this stage that he decides that this other side exists but must not be allowed to gain the upper hand. Thereupon the Creature returns to its element.

At the same time, another of Toft's dreams is put into perspective. It has been obvious from the start that his picture of Moomin Valley and the family living in it is an idealized one, the goal of his aspirations, rather than a picture based on reality. He is even aware of the existence of the magic sphere, though he never really sees anything in it even when he finds it. He views the family with great respect, even awe, though he has no real foundation for this. He is finally disillusioned by Mymble, who tells him outright that Mamma and Pappa have had their disagreements and their black moments, when they would withdraw to the uncultivated forest at the back of the house. At first Toft will not believe this, but with his increasing sense of reality and his new insight into the two sides of his own nature, he does accept a more realistic picture of Mamma. In the final chapter, after the departure of Snufkin, he even goes himself into the trackless forest and there experiences for himself the effect it must have on the others. If the novel is to be seen in a predominantly symbolical light, then this wasteland must represent the hidden, primitive side of human nature with which Toft has now come to terms. Yet another of the characters has gone through a fundamental, traumatic experience from which he has emerged still as himself, but more realistic. Therefore, with his new insight and his new sense of realism, he is the right person to stand on the jetty to receive the family on its return at the end of the book.

If in the course of Toft's story the Creature is to be seen as a projection of the whomper himself, the parallel must be drawn to the figure of Grandpa Grumble, who also literally is attracted by a reflection of himself. Not unlike the fillyjonk, he comes to the Moomin house out of a sense of loneliness, and he, too, has withdrawn from human contact. It is obvious that he is convincing himself rather against his will that he does not want human contact, as he is both difficult and deaf and thus obviously apt to be left out of things. On arriving at the Moomin house, he shows himself to be suspicious and obstinate, convinced that he has the right names for everything, that he is fishing in the right place, that he is well able to eat the food that Mymble warns him off. A hundred years old, he is jealous when he hears of the existence of the "ancestor" who is three times that age, and he makes it his business to find him. He does find him, in his own reflection in the dusty mirror, and the "ancestor" becomes his best friend, politely bowing every time Grandpa Grumble bows and never contradicting. He is a silent reflection of Grandpa Grumble himself, of course, an idealized version of him, who is invited as guest of honor to the great family dinner. When he does not put in an appearance, the rest of the family humor Grandpa Grumble by going to find the "ancestor" in the mirror. They have all seen through the situation, but avoid revealing the secret. Finally, however, after Grandpa Grumble has been obliged to admit that some of the things he has maintained have after all been wrong, and when he visits the "ancestor's" room after it has been cleaned in the fillyjonk's spring-cleaning expedition toward the end of the book, he loses his temper with his silent partner, prods him with his walking stick, and thereby smashes the mirror and the image it contains. Another illusion has been destroyed, and Grandpa Grumble is himself coming to accept the reality of his life.

The last of these characters undergoing a transformation is Snufkin, whose experiences are closely related to those he had in "The Spring Tune," published nine years before. He is again both the artist and the philosopher, again the creature seeking solitude and having to accept that there are other beings around him who make their claims and who to some extent must be satisfied before he can find his melody. Snufkin's experience in "The Spring Tune" is closely tied to the figure of Teety-woo, with whom it is possible to compare Toft in this novel, though, with the larger canvas and the greater number of characters, Snufkin is not seen exclusively in relation to him. The closeness of the parallel with "The Spring Tune" is indicated by the way in which Snufkin in the first chapter quickly and easily puts Moomintroll out of his head in exactly the same way as he did in "The Spring Tune"--though, again as in the short story, he later acknowledges their close friendship and goes to great lengths to find the letter he is convinced Moomintroll must have left for him. Moomintroll has <u>not</u> left a letter for him, any more than <u>he</u> has left one for Moomintroll, an oversight for which he significantly makes amends before going off on his new winter journey.

Again as in "The Spring Tune," Snufkin is less than approachable when he returns to the valley to seek his melody and finds all these strangers instead. Yet he does not send them away, trying instead to keep the peace and occasionally, as when he persuades the fillyjonk to go into the kitchen, actually starting the process that finally leads to their emergence as more balanced beings. For the most part, he says little, but on one occasion he loses his temper--as he has never done before. This is, of course, when the ever-busy hemulen starts putting up the sign bearing the name of the house. In becoming so angry, Snufkin loses prestige to some extent, but he becomes more real and less idealized in his own eyes and those of the other characters. Again one is reminded of his own words in "The Spring Tune" to the effect that it is never good to have too much admiration for anyone. He, too, has his weaknesses.

<u>Moominland in November</u> is not a book for children. In it, Tove Jansson preaches almost directly a greater concern for reality, which, put into literary terms, must mean a plea for greater realism. And that could be achieved only by means of books in which the back-

ground and the characters are more realistic. In reaching this point, she has reached the end of a road that has become more and more obvious since the very early days of the Moomin books. The first two might well have been written for children and only children, but after that there is a tension between the demands of the children's book and the adult book, which does not lead to any kind of literary imbalance, but which the writer must have been keenly aware of. For a long time, she strikes a balance between the two, but in the last two of the series, the balance tips more and more away from the children's book, and more and more toward the adult book. The problems that have come to dominate are those of personality, of old age, of loneliness, of change, of obsessions and fixed ideas, and these are not problems that can adequately be dealt with within the framework of a fantasy world devised for children. It was apparent that if she were to go further in her artistic development, Tove Jansson must move into other fields, and this is what she did.

## Chapter Eleven
## *The Sculptor's Daughter*

In 1968, between the publication of the last two of the Moomin novels, Tove Jansson for the first time wrote a clearly adult novel, The Sculptor's Daughter. The title and the picture of some of Viktor Jansson's sculptures on the front cover tend to indicate an autobiographical work of some kind, but the reader who approaches this book in the hope of learning something concrete about Tove Jansson's childhood will be disappointed. There are very few pieces of tangible information, no dates, few allusions to anything but the child Tove's immediate world, seldom a real indication of who people are if, indeed, they existed at all. Some of the more fantastic episodes are without doubt flights of the imagination and tell more about the workings of a child's mind than what that child actually experienced. Were it not that Tove Jansson herself is the daughter of a sculptor and that the events in this book are narrated in the first person (in itself a doubtful piece of evidence), the reader might be forgiven for wondering whether this is not a novel, or a series of related short stories, about a fictitious sculptor's fictitious daughter, the whole book having certain themes in common with the Moomin books.

**Artistic Setting**

In the Moomin books, from "The Spring Tune" onward, the problems of the artist and of artistic inspiration have never been far away. It therefore seems natural that Tove Jansson should now choose to write an entire book on the childhood experiences of a girl growing up in a predominantly artistic milieu, seeing the world not with an artist's eye but with the eyes of a child for whom art and a reverence for art are part and parcel of her daily life. The child's behavior shows clearly how she accepts as normal and natural the particular way of life that results from being a member of an artist family and at the same time realizes there is something special--<u>sacred</u> is the word used on more than one occasion--about artistic creation.

Even in the first chapter, "The Calf of Gold," the artist's eye is obvious, not so much from the general description, precise and visual as this is, as from an apparently chance comment. Despite its title, this story is as much about a child's desire to assert itself, a story of "dare," as of a calf of gold. Tove, brought up in a religious atmosphere and vying for first place with her cousin, decides to build herself a calf of gold and worship it, in defiance of the accepted norms by which she is surrounded. There is a suitable place for the "calf," a circle of trees planted by her grandfather, which have now grown too big and dark to be used for the shelter from the sunshine for which they were intended. Tove builds her calf in this ready-made heathen grove; the decision to make a calf of gold can be seen as an extension of her father's sculpturing, but this is underlined by an accompanying remark of some significance: " a circular background is always good for sculpture" [10]. Whether this indicates the little girl's awareness of such things, or whether it represents the grown woman's rationalization of her childhood is left to the reader to decide.

Ultimately the story of the calf of gold is not a story about "art." Nor is the next chapter, "Darkness," though a very different version of the art motif can be discerned in it. Tove and her friend Poju are building a secret passage, and here Tove's artistic background comes in useful, as she is able to use one of her father's tools (a hammer for chiseling marble) to further the project: "Poju's hole is much smaller, but his father has such poor tools that it is a pity for him" [18]. Rather like the instance cited above from "The Calf of Gold," this is an example of the artist's daughter taking her artistic background for granted. Her dawning artistic sensitivity also appears in this story, again introduced as a by-product of the artistic home. The secret passage is hidden by a picture her mother did on sacking when a girl:

> It is Mamma's tapestry, which she did on sacking when she was young. It represents an evening. There are some straight tree trunks rising above the marsh, and behind the trunks the sky is red because

the sun is setting. Everything except the sky has darkened to an indeterminate greyish brown, but the narrow red stripes shine like fire. I am very fond of her picture. It goes deep into the wall, deeper than the hole I have made, and deeper than Poju's room; it is never-ending, and you never get far enough to see where the sun is going down, but the red simply becomes deeper. [18-19]

Not only does this passage imply the artistic background, but it is in itself a powerful expression of the experience of a work of art which can be so overwhelming--more than merely realistic--that the person endowed with the right senses can feel it and live it. It is an experience closely related to that described in <u>Moominpappa at Sea</u> when Mamma paints her garden on the wall and then actually disappears into it. The intensity of artistic experience is linked to the imaginative process, another theme that is at the center of this book and of primary importance in Tove Jansson's other work from this time. The author's own imagination and artistic sensitivity are implied in the last paragraph in a brief reference to her father's sculptures: "Pappa's sculptures moved gently around us in the light from the fire, his sad white women who stepped cautiously forwards and were all ready to take flight" [22].

<u>The Sculptor's Daughter</u> is full of such brief references as this last one, but it contains much more than that. The child's awareness of the role of art in her home and of the difference between art and non-art is clearly to be seen in several of the chapters. In "Anna," the somewhat temperamental house helper makes a deprecating reference to the books that Tove's mother reads, and Tove immediately comes to her mother's defense:

I explained to Anna that Mamma can't manage to read any books apart from those she is doing the covers for so that she can know what the book is about and what the heroine looks like. Some just draw as they feel like and don't give a fig for the author. You can't do that. An illustrator has to think of both the author and the reader and sometimes of the publisher as well. [36]

*The Sculptor's Daughter*

She then follows with an explanation of the color techniques that force her mother to paint hair in colors different from what she knows it to be from the text. Whether this is to be seen as a real episode or a later rationalization, it is another example of the artistic awareness that is a constant feature in the book. It appears again in "The Bays," where Tove compares the forest to a drawing by John Bauer [10]; she gives a brief explanation of his technique, says that no one else has ever made a success of it, and adds that she and her mother have despised those who have made the attempt. Once more the episode can be taken at face value, but it can also be seen as an indication of Tove Jansson's own artistic principles, for a comparison between her description of John Bauer's forests and the ones she herself draws in the Moomin books shows a striking similarity of artistic theory.

In two of the stories, "High Water" and "The Visitor," art plays an essential part. In "High Water," the family is seen spending the summer on an island. It is a family picture, but more especially a picture of an artist family, with Mamma sitting on the veranda doing her illustrations and sending them off to Borgå, and Pappa looking for a place to use as a studio. The boathouse is suitable, and he takes it over:

> He made the boathouse into a studio, and everyone was interested and gave a hand. They tried to get Kallebisin's tools out of the way and wanted to wash the floor, but they were not allowed to.
> Pappa became angry, and then they understood that the boathouse had become a sacred place and was not to be touched in any way. No one went down on to the beach any longer, and the boats were left lying by the jetty. [71]

The boathouse thus becomes a temple, something sacred, where Pappa can create his art and where he must not be disturbed. While Mamma goes on with the illustrations, Pappa spends his time in solitude in the boathouse after an early morning fishing expedition. The family knows his need for solitude and respects it, but others do not. As happens in the case of Snufkin in both "The Spring Tune" and <u>Moominland in November</u>, his peace is disturbed by people who have no understanding of or respect for his artistry. Other summer visitors come to watch him, call him "the sculptor" and even, to the horror of his daughter, ask how his inspiration is going: "I have never heard anything so tactless" [73]. Like Snufkin, Pappa resigns himself to the situation, though he becomes more and more somber, until he finally says nothing at all; it is the picture of the frustrated artist.

It is clear that one of the tensions on which this story is based is that between those who understand and appreciate art and those who do not, a distinction so clear that in "Jeremiah" Tove hurls at her grown-up and triumphant rival the worst insult she can think of: she is an amateur, with no sense of art. This is quite an insult for a child! Apart from the fact that the word <u>amateur</u> is likely to be the only one understood by this young foreign woman who has usurped Tove's place and with whom she cannot carry on a conversation, it must be an almost unique occasion in literature that the worst insult a child knows is to call someone else an amateur.

The same tension between the artist and the non-artist is found in "A Visitor with an Idea," another tale of the disturbance to which Pappa was subjected, even at the most solemn moments. If his artistic activities as a whole are thought to be sacred, then the actual process of casting the plaster is one of the most solemn rituals. It is precisely this moment that a visitor chooses not only to come and disturb him but even to start playing with the plaster he is using. Nevertheless, Pappa's human warmth wins over his artistic frustration, and he not only allows her to experiment with some plaster on her own, but actually helps her to make a plaque in which a glossy picture is fixed in the plaster. And this is such a success that the poor woman makes a whole collection of them. The contrast between the glossy, sentimental, and garish pictures and the "real" art created by Pappa is obvious, but Pappa is patient and even allows one of the pictures to be hung in his studio. Tove herself has one and reveals a certain ambivalence toward it, for on the one hand she knows it is not real art, but on the other she is only a child and finds it rather attractive. However, she <u>is</u> concerned because the other woman not only produces non-art but is entirely uninterested in Pappa's "real" art. Behind all this, the reader is aware of Pappa's tolerance and understanding: he never complains, but allows a lonely person to have a little innocent enjoyment.

This woman has certain characteristics in common with a fillyjonk, obviously obsessed with certain ideas; at the end of the chapter she is engrossed in her glossy plaques, but at first she is equally concerned with cementing and decorating some steps. Her lack of insight is such that she cannot even think far enough ahead to fit in all the stones she needs for the last word of an inscription she attempts to produce. When Pappa says he would have helped her if he had known, her impatient reply is that it is easy to be wise after the event. A glaring contrast is inherent between the woman who is incapable of producing a satisfactory pattern out of stones, and Pappa, who even arranges the mushrooms he gathers and the fish he catches in an artistic manner.

**The Imagination**

Side by side with the treatment of the artistic imagination goes a consideration of imagination in general. It is seen in relation to Tove herself, not via any of the other characters. The power of the imagination, which in <u>Moominland in November</u> is related to Toft, is here unambiguously associated with Tove, and the influence one person's fantasies can have on someone else, which in the later work verges on the demonic, is lightly touched on here. Imagination is obviously a dominant factor in "The Calf of Gold," with Tove's determination to build and worship such a calf, but in "Darkness" the power of one person's thought over someone else is unmistakable. Tove succeeds in convincing her playmate Poju that there are snakes under the carpet and that he must keep to the light-colored parts. It is a game much like any child's game of avoiding cracks on a pavement, but Tove manages to terrify Poju:

> If you step out on to the brown you're lost. It's swarming with snakes down there; you can't describe it, only imagine it. Everyone has to imagine his own snake, for someone else's can never be so terrifying.
> He balanced his way over the carpet with tiny

> little steps and with outstretched arms; his big wet handkerchief flapped piteously in one hand.
> "It's getting narrower," I said. "Be careful now and try to jump across to that light flower in the middle." [17]

Naturally enough, Poju falls and is appalled at the prospect before him, and has to be comforted--by Tove.

This episode is obviously related to "A Tale of Horror" from <u>Tales from Moomin Valley</u>, but special interest must be attached to the remark that someone else's snake can never be so frightening. This is illustrated more fully in the Toft episode in <u>Moominland in November</u>: Toft creates the Creature in his own imagination, and he is the only one to be frightened by it or even to experience it. And as though to emphasize this phenomenon, there is another example in "Darkness" of how things grow in the imagination; this time it is the power of words that is the essence.

> Explosion is a beautiful word and very powerful. Later I learned others. . . .
> They become even more powerful if you repeat them time after time. You whisper and whisper and make the word grow until there is nothing but the word. [19]

This is almost a precise definition of what Toft does, and his experience is repeated in "The Tulle Dress." Tove wraps herself up in her mother's tulle dress and sees the world in a new light. She sees herself in the mirror as an animal, and from there her imagination is given free rein: "Outside in the studio the great beast was on the prowl. It multiplied and turned into lots of animals. They sniffed around and found the scent and threw long shadows across the floor . . ." [117].

It is, however, in the story called "The Bays" that the power of the imagination is accorded the fullest treatment. Tove goes out early one morning to visit a number of bays along the coast, and on the way she imagines meeting various people. It is some time before the reader realizes that these encounters are imaginary, as the coastline is described realistically, and the first meeting is at first presented in the same realistic tone. However, it becomes obvious that this and the ensuing meetings are figments of a powerful imagination. The delicate balance between involuntary and willed imagination, which is seen in Toft's tendency not to be able to maintain his mental picture of Moomin Valley at the start of <u>Moominland in November</u>, emerges clearly. Tove meets, in her imagination, one of the pilots based on the coast, and they sit and discuss the world and drink deep of home-distilled spirits and coffee. But then the picture changes:

> After that I could not retain the picture of him any longer.
> It is sad when they become misty and disappear. You say all the right things, but they still disappear. And then there is no point in going on, for it simply becomes silly and you feel so lonely. [52]

Whether this process is to be seen as faltering inspiration or a mental process, the implication is clear that it is impossible to maintain a fantasy picture merely by willing it. The fantasy seems to live a life of its own, to take control of the mind and being at times, but at others to elude a determined effort to produce and govern it. Whether this problem ultimately is the result of the Moomintroll idea getting out of control and making demands is, of course, open to speculation. Perhaps in this respect, there is a deeply felt truth in the words with which "The Tulle Dress" finishes: "I mean, anyone can let dangerous things loose, but the catch is putting them in their place afterwards" [119].

**Affinity with the Moomin Books**

In moving from the Moomin books to an adult novel, the reader will inevitably look for similarities or points of contact. There are many, some surprising, others to be expected. The family atmosphere is very much like that described in the Moomin books, except that Pappa is a much more practical and perhaps a more harmonious being in <u>The Sculptor's Daughter</u>, less concerned with his own position and more sure of his ability to make a contribution to family life. Mamma, on the other hand, is very much the same Mamma, gentle, kind, hospitable. The hospitality of the family is emphasized, and on more than one occasion, it is stressed that they are not merely middle class and respectable. Anna, one of the helpers in the house, actually insults Tove by referring to the family as bourgeois. There are plentiful indications of the relaxed way in which they take things, varying from Pappa's philosophical resignation when the waves ruin the plaster he is about to cast to the early remark that Tove's grandmother had a huge collection of buttons, which she kept carefully arranged until she went bankrupt, after which all semblance of order disappeared: "and that was really nicer" [109]. Likewise there are two passages referring to the difference between a woman and a lady. Tove prefers the former category; her mother belongs to it--she is too full of life to be a lady. Pappa's statues, on the other hand, are ladies. The most Bohemian impression of the family is to be found in the chapter entitled "Party," telling of parties lasting far into the night, during which Pappa plays his balalaika and Cawan his guitar:

> They were gentle and melancholy songs about things that go on and on and which no one can do anything about. Later they became wilder and madder, and Marcus would break his glass. But he never broke more than one, and Pappa made sure that he was always given a cheap glass. . . . I love Pappa's parties. They can go on for night after night, wakening and then sleeping again and draped in smoke and music, and then suddenly a yell enough to send shivers to your feet. [29-30]

This is more unconstrained than anything seen in the Moomin books, but this *is* an adult book, and the relaxed nonchalance is the same, as is the respect the various members of the family feel for one another. When Mamma replaces one of the figures for the crib, the result is not entirely happy: the new figure is the wrong color, and it is too fat--but no one upsets her by telling her so.

Elsewhere the similarities are rather of detail. Some of Tove Jansson's remarks in this book seem to echo Little My, and as though to underline this similarity she once talks of imagining herself to be so small that she could fit into a pocket. There is a discussion between her and her mother on fires, somewhat reminiscent of Pappa's fear of smoldering fires in

*The Sculptor's Daughter*

Moominpappa at Sea. On a different level again, Tove senses in "Jeremiah" that the other girl is afraid when out in a boat: "I saw that she was cold and that she was afraid of the sea. . . . I could see on her hands how frightened she was" [80]. This recalls Toft in Moominvalley in November who is able to sense that the fillyjonk is afraid but not dangerous. In "Anna," Tove goes out with the daily help to fetch bird cherry blossoms from the local park, and her fear of being caught by a park keeper echoes Snufkin's dislike of park keepers and notices saying "Keep Out." The innocent Tove remarks that her father would never have done this, and it is here that Anna replies that that is because he is too bourgeois!

This is the story of a child and her experiences, one of which without doubt is her experience of fear. One can almost talk of a fascination for fear. The fire she discusses with her mother is "a fire like the one Pappa is always expecting." There is a sense of fear in the park when she is out gathering flowers with Anna, and when she is struggling with the "silver" stone up the stairs of the block of flats in "The Stone," especially when she hears someone coming up behind her. There is a nightmare quality in the way this person, the porter, gradually draws nearer, and in the way, when the stone falls over the balcony, <u>all</u> the inhabitants of the flats come to the window and <u>all</u> their doors are opened. It is both nightmarish and stylized, and in a way Tove seems to enjoy her fear. She certainly enjoys it elsewhere: "[I] was so beside myself with fear and delight that I almost wet my pants," she comments in "Anna" [40], and her reaction to the ballad of Hjalmar and Hulda is "You shudder, it is lovely" [35]. Fear is an essential element in "Darkness," and the contrast to this comes at the end of the book, in "Christmas," where the picture is one of "absolute security." The familiar contrast between security and danger in the Moomin books is again present in this first adult book, though the danger now seems to lie in Tove's imagination, never in reality. Even the storm described in "High Water" does not actually bring danger with it, and it is described as one of the best storms Tove has ever known.

In <u>The Sculptor's Daughter</u>, Tove Jansson took her first real step away from the Moomin world she had carefully and painstakingly constructed over the years.

The themes were clearly related, but the very knowledge that these were real people and the world a real world both directed and liberated her imagination. It left her much freer to write on certain aspects of human nature with which she was becoming increasingly concerned, and which only with great difficulty if at all could have been made to fit into the Moomin world.

## Chapter Twelve
## *The Listener*

With *The Listener*, Tove Jansson moved completely away from the pattern she had followed so far. In *The Sculptor's Daughter*, she had left her former world of make-believe, but the family pattern was similar to that in the Moomin books. In *The Listener*, she abandoned that as well and took a further step into the world of free fantasy. This did not mean, however, that there were to be no points of contact with what had gone before--on the contrary.

The title story itself points both backward and forward, back to the obsessiveness of the fillyjonk and forward to the even stronger obsessive tendencies that were to be further explored in *The Doll's House*, the ability of a human being to get lost in his or her own imagination and thus become divorced from time and reality. Personality changes, which had been touched on in the later Moomin books, are taken as the point of departure.

Aunt Gerda has hitherto been kind, understanding, attentive, a rather colorless person who has enjoyed the devotion and confidence of all her relatives. There is no reference to a husband, and one assumes she is unmarried. However, at the age of fifty-five, Aunt Gerda begins to change, to lose her grip, forgetting names, arriving late, being terrified of making a mistake. She herself notices this change, which has come with the years, and she decides to correct it and train her memory again. During her long life of listening to others, she has come to know virtually all the secrets of her relatives, and she decides to make a chart of their lives and careers. It is this chart that becomes her obsession. Not only does she spend all her time and energy on it, but she realizes that she can produce variations on the chart at will, thus reflecting in her imagination changes in the fates of those concerned; for the first time in her life, she has a sense of power over others. Moreover, time--with which she was once very concerned--no longer seems to be of any importance to her: "Now she had time to remember. Time was not dangerous any longer, it went parallel with herself, and sooner or later she would have it fixed in a decorative oval surround" [15]. In creating her own time in this way, she appears to be embarking on the same path as the grandmother in "Time Concept" from <u>The Doll's House</u>, but whereas in the later book Tove Jansson was to allow the grandmother to go on living in her own world, Aunt Gerda is suddenly drawn back into a different reality. When she has completed her chart, she decides to ring her nephew and invite him round to discuss his painting—only to discover that he has long since given up painting and now works for his father. Time has passed, and changes have taken place unbeknown to Aunt Gerda. Her chart has stagnated: it is only a plan of a situation at one particular moment, and it is no longer relevant.

The progress of time was now established as a major motif in Tove Jansson's work; with time come not only new events, but changes in people, in particular old age. Aunt Gerda thus becomes the first of a number of figures at the center of Tove Jansson's adult work; she is an elderly woman, lonely, unable any longer to make contact with others, tending to be obsessive. These are themes that are largely recognizable from the Moomin books—the Groke, the fillyjonks, the hemulens—but they can now be combined in new ways. This short story thus signifies a new departure.

"The Listener" is one of the best stories in the volume which seems to be composed in a series of undulations, with long and important stories alternating with shorter ones—which are not necessarily lightweights. In the three short tales following—"Tipping Sand," "Children's Party," and "The Sleeping Man"—themes appear that are on the whole well-established in Tove Jansson's work. The loneliness of old age portrayed in "The Listener" is followed in "Tipping Sand" by a portrayal of youthful vigor and optimism, a charming, well-observed story in which only at the end is it revealed that the girl shoveling sand is but a child. In "Children's Party," the theme reverts to that of middle-aged loneliness, when two sisters, both unmarried and with little in common, try to arrange a party for their niece, though with little success. Vera, the more pessimistic of the two, remarks that nothing they ever do seems to be a success, and she adds that as far as they themselves are concerned, they never talk to each other, they merely exist together. This pathetic story is then followed by a strange account of how two young people go one night to a flat to attend to someone whom they appear not to know. The girl is afraid, and it emerges that the man is an insomniac who has taken too many sleeping pills. Nevertheless, there is a certain eeriness to the story, a sense of--perhaps unnecessary--fear. The dangerous things that were often referred to in the Moomin books turn up here in different forms.

The next major story is "Black and White," a tale in which the problems of artistic conception are interwoven with those of human relationships. The title refers not only to the illustrations the narrator, an artist, is trying to create, but to the contrast between the house his wife has designed, cold and impersonal, and the one to which he retires to work: it is old and dilapidated, but it is one in which a human being can live and be himself. Stella's house is open and almost entirely constructed of glass; there is no privacy, no doors behind which to retire; on the other hand, there is a wall round the garden to keep out the world outside. Everything is functional and impersonal, and the artist is incapable of creating pictures of character while living in it. They are all gray, and he is unable to add sufficient black to give them effect. Even the table at which he works is made of glass. When he is asked to do a set of illustrations for a book of horror stories, he realizes the impossibility of working under these conditions. His wife, a woman as devoid of human characteristics as the house she has designed, suggests that he should go and work in a villa that used to be owned by his aunt. This he does; he <u>can</u> live in this house, and he <u>can</u> produce the black element of his drawings, the black that seems also to represent the more somber sides of his own nature, the side it is necessary to express in order to express his full self.

Along with this consideration of human relationships and human nature goes the question of artistic creation, the problem of what an artist seeks to achieve. "It is not what is expressed that interests me," thinks the artist, adding that "what is suggested is far more important than what is explicitly portrayed" [49]. It is this ability to suggest, to make his pictures progress from gray to black and represent movement or development that he discovers in the old house. What has obviously been the impersonal nature of the drawings he has produced before gives way to life, movement, depth (1). The illustrations proceed apace and are accompanied by a series of drawings of the old house. There is something obsessive about this new wave of creativity. At last only one picture remains to be done; it must be a frightening picture, and the artist himself is afraid of it. He can achieve the terrifying effect he seeks only by drawing his wife's sitting room, which disintegrates as he comes to the darkest part. The whiteness, the impersonality, of the house and all it represents cannot survive the power of the black element.

The mood changes considerably in the next story, "Letters to an Idol," and the sympathetic description of the principal character, a lonely woman living a life entirely in her own romantic thoughts, is mixed with a touch of gentle irony. For the romantic life she "lives" is far removed from reality. Her idol is a writer of romantic love stories whom she idealizes and fashions in her own mind according to her own concepts. She even dreams of being the woman in whom he can confide. When his newest book is given a bad reception, it does not strike her that there might be a reason; she rereads everything he has written and sends him a letter in which she praises him for the way in which he portrays love as something pure and elevated. As long as she has not contacted him, she has had a strange sense of power over him, but now she realizes that she is exposing herself to disillusionment, that she might be faced with a different kind of reality.

So she is. She finally visits the author, is kindly received by him in luxurious surroundings in which a tiger skin symbolically decorates the floor. The atmosphere is tense, the conversation constrained, the music cold. Finally the front door opens, and the woman decides it is time to go. The new arrival is still in the hall, but she does not raise her eyes to see who it is. This newcomer, however, who is obviously at home, is a man. The woman goes home, still apparently oblivious of the real situation, and falls asleep with her romantic dreams.

While "Letters to an Idol" can be described as an ironical consideration of an obsession, another obsession is treated humorously in "A Love Story." An artist goes to the Biennale in Venice and is overwhelmed by a sculpture of a torso--"in fact a bottom." He becomes obsessed with the idea of owning it. However, he is living on a scholarship, which will be used up on the statue, and he is traveling with a girlfriend who on the one hand appears to be fairly economical, but on the other has very little understanding of art. In the end the girlfriend wins.

It is not clear whether "The Other One" is about a schizophrenic or a wraith, but at all events it fits into a tradition of people who meet their doubles and is also in the pattern of Tove Jansson's fascination with the complexity of human personality. In some stories of this kind, one character seeks to achieve power over another; here, a single character becomes divided into two, even to the extent of talking of himself partly in the first and partly in the third person. The emotions following each meeting between the two are varied, and in the end they are united again. Like other stories in this volume, "The Other One" points the way forward to The Doll's House, especially to the story "Locomotive," where the principal character also takes to talking of himself impersonally in the third person at times. And like this later character, too, the one in "The Other One" is deeply engrossed in an artistic problem reflecting the barren nature of his personality, the design and positioning of letters.

Obsession plays no part in the following three short tales, the first of which, "Spring," is mainly a brief, atmospheric description of the approach of spring, though with the loneliness motif glimpsed in the background through the individual figures and their reactions to spring and sunshine. "The Silent Room" also reflects loneliness. An old man has, presumably, attempted suicide, and while searching for his belongings to take to the hospital, one of the other figures tries to gain some impression of him. In atmosphere, "The Storm" is very much like "The Fillyjonk Who Believed in Disasters," a description of a lonely woman's experience of a violent storm during the night; she is waiting for a man to call her, but when he does so, in the middle of the night at the height of the storm, he is no more than a voice on the telephone promising to ring again the following day. In her way, this young woman is as lonely as the other characters in these three stories.

The mood changes radically in "The Grey Duchess." Manda has second sight, and she can see on people when they are going to die. Moreover, she cannot refrain from telling them. This revelation in the first paragraph of the story produces an inevitability about the rest of it. Manda goes from Ostrabothnia to Helsinki to work as an embroiderer. She is a gifted woman, but she is by nature different from those whom she has to work with, and her isolation is underlined by her working in a glass "cage" of her own, visible to the others but out of contact with them. She tries to avoid meeting any of the customers, but inevitably she does meet one, and equally inevitably it is one who is going to die before using the dress she is about to have made. Manda tells her so. The prophecy is fulfilled, and Manda, who so far has merely been kept at a distance by her colleagues, is now completely ostracized by them. After her day's work, she walks around in Helsinki and sees people hurrying by; many of them are going to die, and she finally withdraws to her own flat, only to discover that she has lost her ability to choose colors for her patterns. Whether any radical change has occurred in her is left to the reader to decide.

The next story is a kind of interlude, a modest tale of a woman who cannot sleep. Yet "Suggestion for an Introduction" contains its own tragedy, the brief portrait of a lonely insomniac who spends the night trying to sleep, or taking first one, then another sleeping tablet, endeavoring unsuccessfully to read, noting all the sounds in the block of flats, looking through the window occasionally, and finally getting up and making a cup of tea, only to discover that she has read the time wrongly. So she goes for a walk in the cold morning air, and having walked round the block once, she does so again and then is ready to start yet another day. The title "Suggestion for an Introduction" suggests a perspective far beyond the immediate sleepless night.

The loneliness motif takes on another form in "Wolves," where it is fused with the motifs of obsession and the difficulty of communicating with others, forming a story of great intensity. The difficulty of establishing contact is represented here in dual form, partly through the purely linguistic difficulty when the unnamed woman looking after the Japanese visitor, Mr. Shimomura, labors under the problem of not having a language in common with him. The fact that he is a painter or black-and-white artist and she a writer appears to indicate further complications in the relationship between the two.

The sense of individual loneliness is accentuated by a visit to the open-air zoo in the snow, with glimpses of a place that under normal circumstances would be full of people and wakeful animals. Now there is snow, and although there are said to be people working on the island, none appears in the deserted zoo; the otherwise busy restaurant is a dismal sight, clearly intended to underline the desolation both of the scene and of the woman's feelings, while the animals ignore the unexpected visitors with whom they have no contact. Shimomura has seen a stuffed wolf in a museum. He has been fascinated by it and has drawn it in a manner reflecting both sensitivity and brutality, and it is because of this that his guide has decided to take him to the deserted zoo. When they find the wolves there is a change of tone, and it is obvious that a climax of some kind is being reached:

> "Mr. Shimomura," she said quietly. She smiled, almost shyly, and showed him the wolves. There were three big cages and a wolf in each. All three were pacing backwards and forwards to the bars, backwards and forwards in a kind of gliding, loping movement; they did not raise their heads. Mr. Shimomura went closer and looked at them.
> 
> The incessant movement of the wolves struck her as appalling. It was timeless, they loped backwards and forwards to the bars week after week and year after year, and if they hate us, she thought, it must be with a gigantic hatred. [119-20]

But this is what Shimomura wants to see, and he studies them, finally indicating that he has caught the "idea" of the wolves. At the end of the trip, the woman guide wonders whether the wolf he will finally commit to paper will be the one he has seen or one he has imagined.

The story is clearly linked to earlier ones, but it also again points the way forward to <u>The Doll's House</u>. There, in "The Monkey," the lack of contact between human beings and animals is essential to the story, whereas in "Locomotive," the dominant theme is that of an obsessive preoccupation with the "idea" of the locomotive; the determination of the narrator in that story to capture in his drawings the "idea" is obviously akin to Shimomura's desire to capture a mental image of the wolf. There is nothing to indicate whether he succeeds.

Again the theme changes in "Rain," but again there is a familiar motif in the loneliness of the aged and the dying, first portrayed dramatically in the headlong rush of three motorboats as, surrounded by pleasure yachts, they carry a dying woman to the mainland, and then philosophically in the old woman's last experiences in the hospital, accompanied by the light and darkness of a summer night, the sound of thunder and the falling rain.

If "Rain" is concerned with the thoughts of someone in old age, "The Explosion," which follows it, reverts to the thoughts of a child. It is one of the more imprecise stories in the book, open to more than one interpretation, indicating rather than depicting the thoughts of a small boy as he accompanies his father and the father's companion to carry out a blasting operation. He is curious and frightened, confident in his strong father but filled with visions of the disasters that can befall him, a lonely child whose mother is dead and whose contact with his father and, in particular, the father's companion is limited. He is perhaps not particularly intelligent, certainly not energetic, and the story conveys a sense of his bewilderment and general feeling of strangeness on his first trip. When everything is ready for the explosion, he is told where to stand for safety, and the question is whether he is afraid or not. The implication at the end, when he leaves his shelter and sees the bits of rock falling as planned, is that he had been afraid for his father, not for himself, afraid in case his mother's prediction of disaster to anyone interfering with God's carefully arranged natural order should be fulfilled. It is a story of the impact of one human being on another and of the impossibility of communicating that influence to anyone else. The boy's world is a closed one, his alone.

"Lucio's Friends," also about the lack of contact between people, is less a story than a character sketch of an Italian friend of the fictitious narrator. No one seems to understand this charming foreigner, and yet everyone likes him, and the final conclusion is that the narrator has felt friendship for him but cannot explain why. The story contains a striking symbol of loneliness and powerlessness in the picture of the icebreaker that is frozen fast, the symbol of human beings unable to function as intended, of their inability to act, of their isolation.

The final story in The Listener, "The Squirrel," is the most elaborate and the one in which the various themes and motifs in the book are brought together. The narrator is a woman living a secluded life on an island; this is how she wants it, yet unconsciously she feels the loneliness of it all. She rather obsessively organizes her days, in particular dividing them into the right times for having a glass of Madeira. All this is disturbed by the arrival of a squirrel, and we are back with the problem of contact or lack of contact between two living beings. For a moment the woman almost wishes the squirrel were a dog, with which it would be easier to establish contact, but then she recognizes the squirrel's independence and tries to respect it. Life changes for her, and she tries partly to see to the squirrel's needs in respect to food and partly to watch it without being seen. However, she fails to understand it, and it chooses to do other things than those she has planned for it.

In the midst of all this, she realizes that she needs supplies, not least of all Madeira, but she gives up all thought of going to the mainland. A boat appears, full of fisherman, and she resents their presence near her island; equally she resents the fact that they leave again without any attempt to establish contact with her. Later in the story, she listens on her walkie-talkie to communications between fishing boats, and almost despairs at not being able to join in or even to attract attention to herself. She is throughout a mixture of someone seeking a solitary life and yet longing for human contact.

The squirrel is her only contact, but it is a very slight one. The "relationship" between the two comes to an end when the squirrel comes uninvited into the sitting room and is responsible for smashing the last bottle of Madeira. Here the narrator explodes in anger: no one has ever before let her down or broken a tacit agreement in this way. She is, unconsciously, seeking to endow the squirrel with human characteristics, an experiment that is doomed to failure.

The final irony is that the narrator sees the squirrel drifting away from the island in her boat and is now cut off from all kinds of contact, real or imagined, with living beings. So she constructs her own reality and starts to write a story beginning with the words: "On a windless day in November, near dawn, she saw someone on the beach" [175]. The rest is left to the reader.

## Chapter Thirteen
# *The Summer Book*

The very title Summer Book gives an indication of the general lightness of touch and happy atmosphere in a work that on the surface seems to be similar in concept to The Sculptor's Daughter. Like the earlier autobiographical fragments and fantasies, this is the story of a little girl, Sophia, and her grandmother, and their summer on an island. The similarity consists not in any identity between the figures in this and the earlier book, but in the way in which a prolonged experience is portrayed by means of a series of episodes with very little to link them apart from the two main figures. And there are only two main figures. Sophia's father is glimpsed occasionally, usually while he is sitting working at his desk--though, as Sophia thinks to herself on one occasion, it is nice to know he is doing that, because then she knows he is there.

### A Child and Her Grandmother

This poetical, lyrical story certainly contains many familiar themes and motifs, but they emerge without the dark overtones of The Listener. The Summer Book combines a child's experience and thought with those of an old woman, a combination of personalities in which the two can meet and within limits understand each other. The child's view of life contains echoes from the Moomin books; the grandmother's belongs to the category of studies of old age; the relationship between Sophia and her grandmother, sometimes harmonious, sometimes almost nonexistent, reflects the question of human contact. At the same time, the island, which has often been a feature in the earlier work, assumes fresh significance as a refuge from modern civilization, although it is actually threatened by modern civilization. It is a living thing, at times personified in the same way as the island is in Moominpappa at Sea.

Sophia, who is based on Tove Jansson's niece, has lost her mother and therefore spends most of her time with her grandmother, based on Tove Jansson's mother. The child is small, the grandmother old, and both are theoretically under a certain supervision because of their ages; however, Pappa is so busy that no one really bothers, and they are thus able to wander about and talk as they please. The author understands both of them, and they understand each other to a degree; the balance between partial understanding and total understanding implied in the book as a whole is maintained by the constant awareness on the part of the reader of the presence of the unashamedly omniscient author who knows and charts the private thoughts of her characters. This emerges already in the first chapter when Sophia and her grandmother come to deep water near the point of the island: Sophia says she wants to bathe, expecting not to be allowed to do so. The grandmother raises no objections, and so with some trepidation she goes into the water, which is deeper than she has been in before and deeper than she is allowed to go in normally. Her misgivings are caused exclusively by her fear that she will not be allowed to go into such deep water, and her thoughts are conveyed directly:

> It's deep, thought Sophia. She's forgotten that I've never swum in deep water without having someone with me. And so she came out again and sat on the rock. [9]

The real point of this brief recapitulation of thought comes a page later, at the end of the chapter, when the grandmother's reaction to the same episode is indicated:

> The first signs of tiredness approached. When we get home, she thought, when we're inside again I think I'll have a nap. And I must remember to tell him that this child is still afraid of deep water. [10]

There is a delightful humor about this brief episode, although in view of Tove Jansson's preoccupation with the limitations to the contact between people it can be seen in a more serious light. Perhaps it is best conceived as a lighthearted treatment of a serious theme.

There is another instance of the same kind toward

the end of the book, though on this occasion the overtones are different, as it is a question of two <u>old</u> people seeking contact with each other and as such points much more directly to the next novel, <u>Sun City</u>. The little family receives a visit; in general they have an ambivalent attitude to receiving visitors, but Verner, who is seventy-five, is welcome as an old friend of the grandmother making an annual call. According to his custom, he brings with him a bottle of sherry, which the grandmother accepts with her customary thanks. She dislikes sherry intensely, but takes it from Verner with a smile in order to please him. It then emerges that Verner himself hates sherry, but he has always brought it for the grandmother because on the first occasion on which he produced a bottle, she was so delighted.

## A Series of Episodes

There is no story as such in the novel, merely a series of experiences which the child and the grandmother share: the bathing in the first chapter; the experience of the strange clump of shrubbery which they call the haunted forest and decorate with all kinds of chance finds in order to make it look even stranger; the visit by the pretty-pretty and well-dressed town girl, who simply does not fit into the surroundings. They build a miniature Venice, and they discuss the existence and nature of God and the prospect of death. They see the encroachment of "civilization" in the building of a new road on the island, and they see other signs of it when a wealthy businessman builds himself a splendid summer cottage on a neighboring island and spoils the horizon. They watch Pappa planting the garden with exotic plants that do not belong to an island in the Finnish archipelago, and they are impressed by his superhuman efforts to keep the garden watered during a drought--though they meet with success only at the moment when the drought ends. There are storms and a violent gale, and there is a day when superstition seems to get the better of Sophia. This happens after a storm which she thinks she has produced by praying for it, and the episode seems to reflect a subject that has emerged on various occasions: the susceptibility of a child's mind to ideas that are beyond its power of analysis. The question of how much

Sophia understands (and she is obviously an intelligent child) and how much she accepts uncritically is one that lies latent in many of the scenes.

The peculiar mixture of seriousness and humor with which this aspect of the child's nature is treated is revealed in one episode when unexpected visitors come to the island. In the chapter entitled "A Boatload of Rascals," a party of merrymakers approaches the island one night, uninvited and unwanted, to the accompaniment of dance music:

> One warm, quiet night in August we heard the deep blast of a trumpet out at sea; like the last trump. Double rows of lights glided towards the island in a gentle curve; the great motorboat purred as only very expensive and fast boats can purr, and the lamps were all colours from bright blue and blood red to white. The entire sea held its breath. [112-13]

Sophia and her grandmother stand and watch the boat's arrival, while the father dresses and goes down to receive the guests. There is obviously a party on board, and the father does not come back to fetch the others. At this Sophia and her grandmother begin to make up stories about how the people on the boat are smugglers who have stolen the boat. Sophia has her doubts about this bit of fiction and asks her grandmother whether she believes it: "Partly," is the answer. However, the invention is embroidered on, and when the father still does not come back, they begin to pretend that he has stayed behind to "save" them. How much they believe and how much they do not believe is not entirely clear, but then Sophia has the idea that the visitors must have drugged her father and that perhaps he has died from the sleeping tablets they have given him. At this, she really becomes afraid. The truth is that the father has joined the party and that the visitors have left behind a box of chocolates for those who were "too old or too young to take part." Eventually, the father spends the following day recovering from a hangover.

Gently amusing, this episode nevertheless betokens an awareness of the susceptibility of the human mind, particularly the minds of the young and the old, to fantastic ideas. In this story of the closeness existing between a grandmother and a granddaughter, the similarities as well as the differences in the reactions of the two to the events around them are particularly carefully explored.

The chapter entitled "Playing at Venice" has similar overtones. Sophia and her grandmother first discuss Venice and wonder what life there was like in times past--and they develop their own fairy-tale version of it, each encouraging the other to go further. Finally, they decide to build a model Venice of their own. Venice dominates all their thoughts and actions for a time, and when a storm comes and washes it away, Sophia is heartbroken. But the grandmother, with the understanding, patience, and self-sacrifice that are characteristic of her, says she will try to save the "Doge's Palace"--and she stays up all night making another one identical to it, doing her best to hide the fact from Sophia that it is a new one and not the one that was swept away. "Sophia examined the palace very carefully. She put it on the bedside table and said nothing" [44]. Does she understand? And has she at her tender age developed the grandmother's ability to gloss things over and <u>pretend</u> she has not noticed? At all events, the building of Venice becomes, for a time, an obsession with them, a gentle parallel to some of the other studies of obsession that are characteristic of this phase of Tove Jansson's work.

In both the episodes related above, there is implicit the question of the imagination taking over: in neither does it really go beyond the limits of consciousness, and only momentarily does it get beyond control, but they both raise the question of the limit between natural, healthy imagination and obsessive preoccupation with a subject. It would, however, be out of keeping with the generally happy atmosphere in the book if an excursion had been made far beyond the borderline between the two. Even Sophia's excessive and obsessive fear of insects is seen in a humorous light, though it, too, is an approach to the study of the irrational and obsessive: "Inexplicable fear is difficult to do anything about" [128].

There is a touch of irony in Sophia's sudden horror of insects, as she herself has been inclined to make fun of a similar fear in another child, the town girl whom they decide to call Berenice:

Sophia flung open the door and came in and said, "She's crying. She's afraid of ants and she thinks

they're everywhere. She's just lifting up her legs,
like this, and stamping and crying, and she daren't
stand still. What are we going to do with her?"
[26]

This entire chapter on "Berenice" has its humorous overtones, as when Sophia surprises her grandmother by announcing that Berenice has dived into the water--but it turns out that she did so only when Sophia pushed her in. And her hair suffers from the salt water! However, as in many of the amusing incidents, there is a more serious aspect to Berenice's visit and her difficulty in adapting to life on the island. She is a carefully and correctly brought up town child who suddenly finds herself in alien surroundings, the guest of a family that is far from the ordinary concept of bourgeois ideals, a family that basically does not want to be disturbed, and that has developed its own easygoing manner of life:

> The fact that Berenice--we'll call her by her secret name--had come to the island brought about complications which no one had foreseen. They had not understood that for all its nonchalance the family on the island was an indivisible unit. The absent-minded way in which they lived and followed the slow progress of the summer had never been geared to the presence of a guest, and they did not understand that the little girl they called Berenice was more afraid of them than of the sea and the ants and the wind in the trees at night. [27]

The island has been in the family's possession for forty-six years, and they have developed a semi-Bohemian way of life, suited to them, during their summer months on it. Therefore they resent the incursions of civilization, to which they are increasingly subjected. There is, for instance, the bulldozer that comes to build a road; in their eyes, it only succeeds in destroying the nature they love. Or there is the wealthy director who buys the neighboring island and sets about equipping himself with all the modern conveniences to which he is accustomed in the city. He is not interested in becoming a part of the island environment, but sees his island as an extension of his city home. It is now an island decorated with notices saying that strangers are forbidden to land on it, the very kind of notice against which the artistic Snufkin reacted in <u>Moominsummer Madness</u>. Such prohibitions have previously been unknown in a community in which everyone respected one another. Every incursion into the family privacy is, to some extent, resented, and even while Berenice is on her visit, she experiences the grandmother's desire to avoid strangers (though it is perhaps partly explained through her wish to overcome Berenice's own feeling of being a stranger). A boat is seen approaching, and the two hide from what the grandmother calls "the rascals":

> "Why are they rascals?" whispered Berenice.
> "Because they come and disturb us," replied Grandmother. "We are people who live on an island, and everyone else coming here can keep away." [30]

The strategy succeeds, and Berenice does join in the game--which nevertheless really implies a wish to be left alone.

Yet even here, on the island, new ideas begin to assert themselves, and the father decides to introduce plants and bulbs that are not native to it. He does so just after Sophia has been thinking of people living on islands closer to the mainland, building summer houses, and attempting to extend "civilization":

> Yet those poor people living on the green islands nearer the mainland have to console themselves with a bourgeois garden where they set their children about the weeding and carrying water until they collapse. But a little island looks after itself. [101]

However, then comes Pappa with his catalogues of plants and flowers, and then comes the attempt to produce a garden artificial to the island, with Dutch bulbs and red and white water lilies. In his effort to ensure water for these plants, he dams a natural pond, which makes the water rise twenty centimeters: "And the junipers don't like that," thinks the grandmother. The balance of nature is being disturbed, and although it is a joy to see the flowers appearing, there is the subsequent ironical description of the father's great efforts to bring fresh water to the island during a drought in order to save the plants that do not belong there. The island wants to be left alone, as does the island in <u>Moominpappa at Sea</u> when Mamma tries to cultivate it.

All this implies change, and here, as in the works preceding, the question of change is of central importance. The world outside is changing; in August, life on the island begins to change as autumn approaches and preparations are made for the winter and the move to the city. However, even this is not without its consolation:

> Grandmother had always liked the great change in August, perhaps most because of the unchanging course it took, for everything had its own place and could not have any other. It was the time when all traces had to be removed and, as far as possible, the island was returned to its natural state. [155]

However, parallel with the changes on the island go changes in human beings. In particular this is reflected in the personality of the grandmother herself. She is old and is undergoing the changes that come with old age, partly able to understand a child better than people in middle age (very little is actually seen of the father), and yet tiring quickly, obviously suffering from some heart trouble. The closeness and yet the distance between Sophia and her grandmother is clearly seen in the chapter called "The Tent," when the grandmother tells Sophia what it was like when she used to sleep out in a tent as a child. She can no longer do this, but she can allow Sophia to try it for herself. Sophia is not exactly happy alone out there in the tent, and so she goes inside and awakens her grandmother, who patiently lights a cigarette and settles down to talk to her granddaughter:

> "I mean," said Grandmother, "that things shrink and slip back, and that what was fun once isn't important any more, and that is a sad feeling. Thankless in some way." [78]

And later:

> "Oh," replied Grandmother, "I only said that when you're as old as I am and there are lots of things you can't take part in any longer. . . . I've been

able to take part for an awfully long time, and I've seen and lived with all my heart, and it's been unbelievable, I'll tell you, unbelievable, but now it's as if everything was slipping away from me, and I can't remember and I'm not interested, and yet now's the very time I ought to need all that." [79]

Of course, Sophia does not really understand what her grandmother is talking about, but in this mixture of an old person's mental ability to appreciate a child's excitement coupled with her physical inability to do so, there is a certain melancholy entirely in keeping with the general view of old people in Tove Jansson's recent work. Time and again in this book, old age makes its mark on events, either because the grandmother cannot take part in what is going on, or because she needs to rest, or because she cannot really remember. The visit of Verner is almost entirely devoted to the reminiscing of two old people:

"How're your legs?" asked Verner.
"Not so good," was the heartfelt reply. "But sometimes I can get around on them all right." Then she asked him what he was doing at the moment.
"Oh, all kinds of things. . . ." Suddenly he burst out: "And Backmansson's gone!"
"Where's he gone to?"
"He's no longer with us," explained Verner irritably.
"Oh, he's dead," said Grandmother. She began thinking of all the euphemisms for death and the frightened taboos which had always interested her. It was a pity you could never start a reasonable conversation on the subject. They were either too young or too old, or else they hadn't time. [122-23]

Verner continues with complaints that are not entirely unlike some of the grandmother's own, but she has difficulty in accepting them here, partly, perhaps, because she sees them as an expression of old age on the part of Verner. She accepts that she is becoming old, but she wants to do so with dignity, and signs of the helplessness of old age worry her: "When Grandmother was going to sleep she remembered the pottie under the bed and thought how she hated this symbol of helplessness. She had only taken it out of kindness" [158].

Yet she is no longer able to tell stories as she used to: "If I don't tell stories because I want to tell them, then they're no good; they shut down and then I can't find them later" [76]. She is conscious that she has less contact with other people than she used to have and less than she would wish to have, and the only person who is willing to devote time to her is the granddaughter Sophia. In her way, the grandmother is able to introduce Sophia to life, and they experience many things on similar levels. However, after her forty-six summers on the island, the grandmother is now fundamentally unwilling to make contact with others, and indeed, at times even her contact with Sophia seems to fail. Nevertheless, after visiting the new residents on the neighboring island and seeing Sophia's awkwardness, she is quick to realize that Sophia must not be allowed to grow up without contact with other human beings, even if she does live in an island idyll of her own. There are times when the solitary life on the island takes on symbolical form, representing the potential loneliness of the individual.

The balance between deliberate solitude and unwanted loneliness is underlined in the conversation between the grandmother and the new rich neighbor, Melander:

> "Solitude," said Grandmother, "is a luxury."
> "It develops you," said Melander. "Doesn't it?"
> Grandmother said yes it did, but you can also be solitary together with other people, and that's more difficult. [89]

This conversation is essential to an understanding of the author's treatment of the question of solitude and loneliness. Perhaps there is a slightly romantic tinge to the concept of the island as a place that makes it possible to withdraw from civilization. Yet another such artistic expression may be seen in the description of the hermit in his tent in the desert, reading a book with a lion watching over him in the background--a reference to one of Robert Högfeldt's watercolors (1). However, the loneliness resulting from not being able to make contact with other people is a very different matter, one from which the grandmother certainly suffers on more than one occasion.

 <u>The Summer Book</u> has the lightest texture of any of Tove Jansson's books. There are serious themes in it, but only a few of the somber overtones that are so often present in her mature work; even the obsessions in it are only small ones. It is in a natural line of development from <u>The Sculptor's Daughter</u> and has certain affinities with the Moomin books, although the family pattern here is different. At the same time, it is an extended study of certain aspects of old age, and as such, it provides a transition to the next work, <u>Sun City</u>, which concentrates almost entirely on that subject.

## Chapter Fourteen
## *Sun City*

"To feel sorry for people means understanding, and if you understand people you can't help liking them." These words from the novel <u>Sun City</u> sum up the author's attitude throughout this tragicomical story of the residents of Butler Arms, one of many private homes for old people constituting the raison d'etre of St. Petersburg, Florida. In writing this book, Tove Jansson focuses on the unpredictable behavior of old people and the lack of contact between them, with the obsession motif never far in the background. She portrays old people with insight and sympathy, with gentle humor tempered with understanding, and she contrasts them with a young couple who represent the hopes and aspirations of a different generation.

**An Array of Old People**

Like the other adult works, this consists of a number of loosely connected episodes rather than a consistently developed single plot. It is an impression of the everyday lives of the residents, their petty quarrels and limited aspirations, their attitudes to such events as a spring ball and an outing to Silver Glades, their attempts to reconcile themselves to the brevity of the life left to them and to the ever-present possibility of death. As an accompaniment to this, there is a love story centered on Joe and Linda, which forms in a way the framework for the entire novel in that Joe throughout is waiting for a letter from the Jesus People inviting him to Miami. The letter comes at the end and he departs. One aspiration at least is fulfilled, whereas the remainder of the characters in the story continue their uneventful lives, marked more and more by the atmosphere surrounding them. As the story proceeds, Joe's motorcycle forms a constant background, while his quiet love affair with the gentle Linda forms a conscious contrast to the querulousness of old age that characterizes most of the main figures.

One of these figures comments: "Sometimes I can be fascinated by the new elements which in old age add new colours to a familiar pattern" [159]. With these words, Mrs. Rubinstein emphasizes one of the points that have emerged in the course of the novel, which is that many if not all the characters in it are slightly exaggerated or caricatured versions of their former selves. Just before this, Mrs. Rubinstein has made another remark that throws the life in Butler Arms into its proper perspective: "Meanwhile, I have said to myself that you can presumably note the same human passions, misconceptions and lack of purpose in your own surroundings" [159], hinting that the Butler Arms is really a microcosm, a slightly larger than life version of what takes place outside. That Mrs. Rubinstein thereupon immediately reveals that she is losing her memory merely serves to add an ironic touch to a letter that otherwise expresses some of the deeper truths in the book. Miss Frey, the Butler Arms secretary, puts another perspective on it: "I live in a nursery. . . . No one knows how much cruelty there is in a nursery" [30]. The ability of mature human beings somehow to restrain their baser instincts has disappeared here, just as it has not developed in childhood. Senility leads to quarrelsomeness and sometimes cruelty, and it is impossible to put a stop to it; it all results from base instincts over which the old no longer have any control, though some may think they have.

The one most fully convinced that she is still in possession of her mental faculties is doubtless Mrs. Rubinstein, but in fact, she, too, is showing signs of decay. She is the domineering person who has spent all her life telling others—not least her son Abrascha, to whom she writes the letter quoted above—what to do. She is insistent that what she wants is the right thing, and she is quick to agree with the owner of Butler Arms, Miss Ruthermer-Berkley, that Miss Frey is not a great success and that she, Mrs. Rubinstein, could probably organize things better. With what results one dare hardly imagine, though the fact that she has been voted off the committee of the Seniors Club does indicate something. The overanxious Miss Peabody at one time strikes up a kind of friendship with her with the remark that she has always admired her, but "you are a hard and dangerous woman" [88].

Others point to her as being domineering, while the impression one has of her at the beginning of the novel is of a fearless, outspoken woman who sometimes goes beyond the bounds of what is permissible. In one of the very first scenes, when the various characters are being introduced, there is a first glimpse of Miss Frey, the frustrated and temperamental secretary, handing over a letter to Mrs. Rubinstein and making the mistake of speaking condescendingly to her, in the tone "which is sometimes used for very small dogs and other people's children: 'A little letter! The postman's brought a little letter for you!'" Mrs. Rubinstein's reaction is devastating:

> The large, dark-eyed woman slowly turned half round and caught Miss Frey in her gaze, surveying the worn features under the wig; she looked down, equally slowly and considered the letter without taking it. They knew she was going to be rude again now. Miss Frey's hand had started to tremble, and finally Mrs. Rubinstein spoke. With devastating graciousness she said: "My dear Miss Frey. My own little letter with my own little brochure inside. For plastic. My modesty, Miss Frey, only my modesty forbids me to say what you can do with that letter." And she added a short, sharp laugh which left Miss Frey in no doubt as to where she could put the letter. [11]

Miss Frey manages the situation and withdraws. Others are less fortunate with "this female sophist," as Mrs. Morris calls her [64].

Nevertheless, Mrs. Rubinstein herself is far from being as secure as she pretends to be. She applies her sophistry to herself in justifying her love of good food, arguing that it becomes more important to eat well as you get older, although she feels that eating for pleasure is despicable. She has one good meal every day, goes to the restaurant by taxi, and keeps the taxi waiting while she eats her meal and thinks of Abrascha, "that fat, silent child which her love had given too much to eat" [80]. However, her insecurity or approaching senility is shown when she spills on the tablecloth and virtually panics in case the waiter should discover it.

None of the other inhabitants resembles Mrs. Rubinstein, but they represent various human types who have come together in this "guest house." Miss Peabody is the diametrical opposite of Mrs. Rubinstein, nervous, with a sense of always having done the wrong thing (which is often indeed the case), and in a way self-assertive. This mixture of self-assertion and nervousness and an inverted desire to attract attention to herself is not entirely unlike the character of Sniff in the Moomin books, and her early remark in connection with the spring ball that "everyone dances at their own risk" is reminiscent of one of Sniff's favorite sayings. (In fact, there is a notice to this effect posted in the club.) Thompson sees her as "a timid, self-centred mouse, without a chin and with whisps of white hair in her head" [20], a description that could well apply to an aged Sniff. Miss Peabody is indeed consistently portrayed as self-centered and possessed by a sentimental desire to relive her childhood, though the author is by no means without understanding for her: "The smell of wet grass and the sound of falling rain took her far back in time and she reminisced without any sense of pain. As always, she thought of her father. She loved him" [53]. Tove Jansson has here sympathetically caught the rather pathetic little woman in the tendency to resort to early memories that is often a feature of old age.

There is, however, a little more irony in the way in which Miss Peabody's reaction to the arrival of Tim Tellerton, the former cabaret singer, is portrayed. She is overwhelmed that a famous star should be coming to live next door, and she thinks of holding some kind of reception for him on his arrival, but is put firmly in her place by Mrs. Rubinstein, who brutally points out that he is coming to St. Petersburg for the same reason as the rest of them--because he is now an old man. "Peabody stared at her without understanding and turned her frightened eyes towards Miss Frey. . . . 'But he's handsome,' said Evelyn Peabody hesitantly. 'He's a great artist'" [85-86]. She is, of course, living in the past, and Tellerton is neither particularly good-looking now, nor is there really any sign that he has been a great artist. But he is the object of Miss Peabody's devotion, her idol, so she sends flowers to him and arranges to have him invited to the ball-- and then does her best to avoid him. Here, as in many other cases, she acts impetuously and regrets it. "Sometimes life was absolutely awful, and it seemed to be at its worst when she had tried to be kind" [117]. The potentially most dangerous thing she does is to warn Thompson that his wife has turned up after looking for him for eighteen years, a warning that has a devastating effect on the old man: in the short run, he disappears and there are fears for what might have become of him; in the long run, it changes him and he never really recovers from the shock. It is not clear whether Peabody has acted on impulse or indirectly wants to see a dramatic event in an otherwise undramatic life; most probably she has acted from sheer thoughtlessness. Her thoughts center only on herself, and everyone knows that she never listens to what is being said. Tellerton is surprised at this, Thompson infuriated.

Thompson is himself one of the sharply defined figures in the novel, a misogynist who torments and terrifies Miss Frey, but will occasionally allow Miss Peabody to go to a bar with him (and let her pay). He subsequently turns out to be married, obviously to a wife who has dominated him. It then becomes clear why he is so difficult as a person, for he is obviously seeking to assert himself vis-à-vis the other residents, having previously been ruled by his wife and, it seems, by his mother. When his wife appears, he takes flight, but he does not, as people fear, either have an accident or go away altogether: "Meanwhile Mr. Thompson was asleep under a thick bush in the town park. This bush had often reminded him of the shrubbery behind his mother's house, where he often hid from her and her sisters" [132]. This is the explanation of his loneliness and aggressiveness, and although he is often portrayed in a humorous light, this shows the true tragedy of a lonely old man who has been subject to strong-willed women all his life and has therefore fled and found himself a corner in a guest house full of women whom he can annoy or terrorize. He also likes to anger other men, and one of his moments of triumph is when he discovers how to irritate Johansen, the odd-job man in the Butler Arms: "He became more and more inventive; he was never allowed to borrow anything, but his questions introduced fear into Johansen's world . . . poisoned his quiet walks around Butler Arms" [39-40]. When the hibiscus blooms, Thompson steals all the flowers and fixes them to the dashboard of a car. Miss Frey, who is the object of his attention in this case, complains to Miss Ruthermer-Berkeley, but despite her ninety years, the owner of Butler Arms advocates tolerance:

> "Dear Miss Frey, we musn't be too hasty. This can't be labelled as what we call a disturbed mind." She looked long at her hands, as she often did at moments of difficult decision, and explained that the borderline between normal irrationality and complete mental confusion is very difficult to define. "We can't know which paths the thoughts and fancies of old people will take." [40]

The remainder of the conversation is of central importance to the novel, underlining the difficulty of distinguishing between normal and abnormal and stressing again that the world outside is not at all that different:

> "But how do we know!" exclaimed Miss Frey. "How do we know where one stops and the other starts? He might burn the whole house down one day!" Miss Ruthermer-Berkeley dismissed this by saying that absolute knowledge is inconceivable, and it was left at that. Afterwards she thought how right it was to press on in view of her age and her insight. She would take care of the irrational products collected over a long life; she considered it a natural product of experience and therefore something which could be explained, nothing to cause concern. . . . Outside St. Petersburg you would come across all kinds of insanity running about loose, and it was no good trying to do anything about that. "But I have built a house for the madness that is innocent, and there it shall be left in peace as long as I live." [41]

### Dreams and Aspirations

Thompson is not allowed to smoke in his room, but he does so as an act of defiance in what is called his last bastion against the world, the cheapest room in Butler Arms. There he can sit at his window and look out on a tiny bit of the world outside, which he begins to transform in his imagination: "Thompson invented a new game: his world was a jungle. The jungle outside

his window became deeper and deeper. . . . The idea of
the world as a jungle brought comfort to Thompson"
[137].

With this we come to an unusual aspect of Tove
Jansson's writing, a central motif of the jungle, which
recurs on many occasions and gradually almost takes on
symbolical value. In particular, it is associated with
Thompson and with Linda and Joe, though it appears in
other contexts, notably in connection with the outing
to Silver Springs and, just before this, the visit of a
Scotsman called McKenzie, who makes a single appearance
on his way to Yucatan, which he proposes to visit
alone:

"Into Yucatan?"
"A little way, only so far that I have been in a
real jungle." [149]

For Linda and Joe, the young lovers, the jungle is
also something desirable, and even if Linda's hope of
making love to Joe in the jungle is not fulfilled, the
visit there and their ecstatic experience of it, followed by their swim in the river with its overtones of
baptism, is one of the climaxes of the novel.

In all these cases, it seems that the jungle represents a dream, an ideal, perhaps some fundamental urge
or instinct in the person experiencing it, and it is
perhaps hardly without significance that Thompson suddenly leaves the jungle path and disappears into the
undergrowth. Until the very end of the novel, the
reader suspects that he has met his death in this
luxuriant but watery dream world, but he is found, and
the only reference made to him subsequently is that he
has been the cause of trouble. Nevertheless, he has
given in to his urge to get away from the trite surroundings to which he is accustomed, an urge parallel
to that of Joe and Linda, who are last seen swimming
naked in the river through the jungle of which Linda
has dreamed so much.

There is without doubt something cultic about this
act, a promise of life, a baptism, though without the
overtones of the Jesus People's baptism in the sea at
Miami. That Joe is known subsequently to go to Miami
is of less consequence when seen in this perspective.
Here, in the jungle river, he and Linda are united in
their cultic act; they cannot, however, be united in

Joe's infatuation with the Jesus People, for Linda is a Roman Catholic, and they have only a limited understanding of each other's religious beliefs. Joe respects the Madonna, we are told, but he is more interested in Jesus, whereas Linda has an altar with a Madonna in her room. A lamp burns in front of it, and Linda prays to Our Lady, a prayer centering on her desire to make love to Joe on the banks of the jungle river: "Afterwards, in your grace, we will wade out into the water and swim together, further and further away" [23].

There is peace, resignation, confidence in Linda's faith, which radiates around her and makes her loved by all, including even Mr. Thompson. Joe's fascination for the Jesus People, on the other hand, is less peaceful, less tolerant, less down to earth than Linda's faith. She resigns herself to that, too, accepting that he will be going to Miami and giving up his job: "Everyone must decide for himself, and those who want to go musn't be stopped" [45]. Joe does go in the end, without Linda, and it is not clear whether he comes back. He is time and time again tormented because he has failed to defend his Saviour, and when he does try to communicate his faith to Tellerton, he fails miserably.

**Human Contact**

Whatever the feelings between Linda and Joe--and they are portrayed with warmth and poetry--there is a limit to how far they can understand each other. They represent in their way part of the study of the limits placed on contact between human beings. That there is a limit to the contact and understanding between the aged in Butler Arms, who have been thrown together by chance rather than choice, is not surprising, but it is significant that Tove Jansson also looks at the extent to which two people who are deeply fond of each other can understand. That limit is here indicated rather than explored.

However, in the case of other characters, it is far more clearly defined, as in the episode referred to above when Joe and Tellerton have a serious talk. A curious friendship arises between Joe of the Jesus People and Tellerton, the former revue actor. There is on the part of some of the characters a certain ambivalence toward Tellerton, though Tove Jansson, with her usual insight into the artistic mind, manages to show understanding even for this kind of artist. Tellerton feels some interest in Joe and mistakenly tries to persuade him not to waste his time, but as time is of no consequence to Joe with his belief in an imminent Second Coming, he has little hope of success. He has to accept this and realize that Joe will neither accept nor reject what he says, but merely see it as something an old man has said. He continues his vain attempt to make contact but has to admit the position to himself: he has neither the strength nor the patience to carry on a conversation with young people. "What is a conversation, what might it imply? A common consideration of important things. Communicating things remembered and things experienced, building ideas for the future" [146]. Even so, he persists, mistakenly giving Joe a book telling of the careers of people who have come from nothing. It is scarcely the book for Joe, who cares for neither career nor time and makes no secret of it. The conversations between them continue, but without result: their fields of experience are too different. There is no contact beyond a certain human warmth.

This is the novel's most direct treatment of the difficulty of human beings' establishing contact, but the lives of the old people point in the same direction. There is Miss Peabody, who never listens to others; there is Mrs. Morris, who at one time resorts to writing messages on slips of paper instead of talking; there is Mr. Thompson, who can be deaf when it suits him, so that it is impossible to make him hear anything; and there are the Pihalga sisters, who never speak to anyone but always sit together reading and who die within half an hour of each other.

While the older residents on the whole are not worried about the lack of contact, there is Miss Frey, who needs to make contact, but cannot, in the course of her duties. In a way she is one of the loneliest people in the novel. She is younger than most of the residents in Butler Arms, and only Joe and Linda appear to be younger than she. She is sensitive to the lack of contact, and she feels overlooked, partly, perhaps, because she is inefficient, but partly because of what she feels to be the futility of it all. She lacks personality whatever she undertakes; she realizes it, and her attempt to overcome the obstacle results in aggressiveness at certain times and irritability at others. Consequently, she lives in a kind of love-hate relationship with Miss Peabody, resulting from mutual insecurity and Miss Peabody's tactlessness, and she is an easy prey for Mr. Thompson's teasing. However, like the others, Miss Frey goes along the jungle path at Silver Glades, and when Thompson disappears she pursues him into the jungle proper, an action that is surely not without significance if the jungle has the symbolical value referred to above. Perhaps she, too, has her own dream world, a world into which she flees from her reality, part of which is some kind of stomach ailment that she is too frightened to consult a doctor about, but which is referred to with increasing frequency as the novel progresses. Like the others, she can be filled with an obsession, as when she desperately tries to find a hairdresser on the day of the spring ball: "As time went on . . . Miss Frey forgot her worries and surrendered herself to the secret obsession, the magic, which female charm gives to the care and attention devoted to her own hair" [94]. She is a tragic figure in that she does not have the excuse of old age for her peculiarities, though she can, of course, be seen as a living example of how little difference there is between the world of Butler Arms and the world outside.

One particular controversy between Miss Frey and Thompson is of special significance, as it touches on another essential theme in the novel: the attitude of the various characters toward death. A storm is approaching, and the residents begin to talk of typhoons; Mrs. Higgins tells of one that left people stuck in the branches of palm trees. Thompson is quick to take up the subject and ask whether they were in bits, only to be put in his place by Miss Frey's very brief, "They were dead." Thompson persists so long that Mrs. Rubinstien calls him phenomenal. Thompson, deaf for a moment, does not hear. To talk about death is one of Thompson's methods of teasing the other residents: "It had been an interesting morning. Every time he had mentioned death one or other of the women had behaved irrationally" [28]. However, some of them scarcely need him to set their minds going in that direction. Miss Peabody is almost obsessed with the idea of death and suffering; even the sight of young people dancing can fill her with thoughts of death: "For an irrational moment she had the thought that they presaged death, as though they were death itself" [112]. Her concern with the subject even forces her to see as a sign of death the cross that Joe has painted on the back of his motorcycle and that for him is the symbol of eternal life.

Mrs. Morris, too, has thoughts on death, even if she is more philosophical. She tries to comfort Miss Peabody, though she betrays some emotion herself: "'Yes,' replied Mrs. Morris testily. 'You can die at any time, but that's not all the world. . . . It simply comes to an end, and for people of our age it can hardly take long'" [73]. She believes that in dying one should try not to frighten other people. The Pihalgas sisters do indeed die in this fashion, though the Mayor is not so fortunate when he collapses of a heart attack during the spring ball. The only other person to share Mrs. Morris's calm is Linda. She expresses some anxiety about going on the back of Joe's motorcycle, and Mrs. Morris immediately concludes that she might be afraid of being killed. Nothing could be further from the truth, and Linda explains with some amusement that she simply dislikes machines. Here again, Linda is the healthy opposite of the old people, seeing things in the perspective of youth. Mrs. Rubinstein also sees death symbols, but she expresses them in her usual self-confident manner when Johansen drives the coach to Silver Springs and she compares him to Charon.

<u>Sun City</u> is unique among Tove Jansson's books. For some time, subjects like old age, obsession, change, human contact have been in the foreground of her work, and here she has fused them together in a novel which has moments of pathos as well as of humor, which is not blind to the commercialization and superficiality of the life offered to the old people, and which indirectly looks at the value of what people achieve in life, whether they be Miss Frey or Tom Tellerton or Mrs. Rubinstein. The reader is left with the feeling that perhaps Linda's calm, unassuming, and gentle approach coupled with her uncomplicated warmth is the author's view of what is best.

## Chapter Fifteen
# The Doll's House

The Doll's House stands in stark contrast to the books immediately preceding it and is far more closely related to The Listener in mood and content than to any of Tove Jansson's other work. It probes the darker recesses of the mind and aims at producing fear in its reader. It is without doubt Tove Jansson's most powerful work to date and is characterized by a new intensity and a new depth of understanding.

"The Monkey," the first story in the book, is the shortest and most optimistic, although even here the optimism is slightly tinged with melancholy. An ageing artist gets up one morning and as usual reads his newspaper, which he is "helped" to do by his pet monkey, who jumps through it. The review of his latest work is negative, though the critics treat him condescendingly rather than harshly; he is himself aware that he is in decline. He carries out a number of aimless tasks, then sleeps for a time, and then takes the monkey out with him to have lunch with some of his fellow artists. Their comments are bitingly sarcastic, and the mood affects the monkey--which has already been infected by the sculptor's own restlessness. They leave, and the monkey finally makes off up a tree; the sculptor does nothing to stop it, only remarking that it may be cold, but at least the monkey can climb, a final comment intended to indicate that the monkey in a way serves as an inspiration to him to have another try.

Although the artist thus derives something positive from the monkey, the idea of limited contact between two living beings is taken to its farthest limit in the portrayal of the relationship between the man and the animal: they are used to each other and the sculptor knows the monkey's habits, but a closer contact between the human being and the monkey with the "expressionless" eyes is impossible. Yet the monkey is susceptible to atmosphere, sensing the sculptor's own mood in the morning, reacting to the teasing of the children on the way to the café and even more violently to the teasing of the critics. It is an outsider. So, in his way, is the ageing artist, as he gradually feels his diminishing artistic ability. Here, then, is a special instance of the artistic problem, a brief and unsentimental look at the artist who is losing his grip.

This is followed by the title story, "The Doll's House," in which the central character, Alexander, is a carpenter and decorator. He is described as a man with a highly developed sense of taste and an unfailing sense of aesthetic values. He shares a flat with a friend, Erik, and when they both come to retiring age, the harmony that existed between them is put to the test. While Alexander succumbs to his creative bent and starts fashioning a doll's house, Erik, far more earthbound, sees to the food. The kitchen has to be divided between them, and Alexander finally is overcome by the obsession of building the house--which in the course of the story becomes the House. He is a perfectionist, bordering on the fanatical, and he cuts himself off more and more. When the telephone rings, it is now described as being like a sound from another world. Alexander has created his own world, and there he is content to live.

Meanwhile, this spoils the contact between Alexander and Erik, who is less at home in this world. He lacks the artistic gifts of his friend, and when he finally does take a hand in things, it is only with limited success. He is forced out to an ever-increasing extent, and this process is accentuated with the arrival of an electrician, Boy, who helps Alexander and becomes as obsessed with the whole idea as he is. Erik resorts to the television, and his estrangement from his closest friend is underlined by the fact that the hatch between his kitchen and Alexander's workshop is closed while Alexander and Boy are working in there, with the result that Erik can hear the drone of their voices but not distinguish the words.

It becomes obvious that some change is coming over Erik, that a crisis of some kind is approaching. It comes when Boy finishes the tower on the house and shows it to Erik, referring to it as "our house." Erik rejects the implication that it is "theirs" and virtually goes amok, attacking Boy with a metal drill and injuring his face; he threatens to destroy either the house or Boy. He is obviously on the borderline of insanity in his despair at being estranged from his lifelong friend, but a simple, everyday movement--that of taking off his spectacles--brings him to his senses. Alexander returns and understands the implication when Erik says he has saved "our home," and he retrieves the situation by remarking that there never was such a house as Erik's and his.

The story centers on the artistic problem again, though this time it is represented by a skilled craftsman rather than an artist proper. He is at all events a man who is seized by a project and cannot leave it alone. Alexander even gets up in the night to go to his House, and he eats his breakfast in his workshop. His obsessive preoccupation with his project creates a barrier between him and Erik and is itself the result of the need to adapt to the change in life-style resulting from retirement. As in <u>Sun City</u>, the innate characteristics of a person emerge more clearly in old age. Alexander even fails at one time to perceive the borderline between reality and fantasy, and he comes close to infecting Erik with his ideas: Erik takes a look at the house's kitchen, typically, of course, for the man who spends his time preparing food in real life, and notices that there is a wood fire in it:

> "Of course. It looks nice."
> "Good Lord," said Erik. "I can't imagine a wood fire. It's no use. Not when you're used to a modern kitchen."
> "You'll get used to it," said Alexander.

A tragicomedy, this story is nevertheless compelling and thought-provoking. The drama develops consistently and constantly until the climax is reached a couple of pages from the end. At one point, it looks as if the outcome will be tragic, but this is prevented by an ordinary action which reasserts everyday reality and breaks through the charged atmosphere that has gradually built up.

The borderline between the real and the unreal is even less clear in the next story, "Time Concept," a whimsical tale of an elderly grandmother with no sense of time who pesters her grandson by giving him a cup of tea in the middle of the night or trying to get him to go to bed at six in the morning. However, this timeless world of hers is skillfully combined with a different time pattern when she and the grandson travel over the North Pole to Anchorage, to the accompaniment of the time changes that take place on such a journey. When they arrive, there is a red glow in the sky, and Lennart, the grandson, remarks that the sun is rising:

> "No, dear, it's setting," replied the grandmother. "That's what's so interesting. Here we come out of a long arctic night, and when we get here the day has already turned into evening." [36]

And she is right. Her complete lack of a sense of time has here won over the grandson with his acute sense of it. The implication may well be that it does not matter in any case.

Time concepts and misconceptions are scattered throughout this story, including the ideas of having enough time or of being short of time. In contrast to the grandmother with her indifference to time comes the rush and bustle in the airport in Anchorage, where everyone is hurrying as though every second counted. The grandson's own sense of time no longer works after his watch symbolically stops on the way--after which there is a surprising change from a first-person to a third-person narrative.

For her part, the grandmother has, in Lennart's own words, created a world within herself, a world in which she is happy and can thrive, and when he seeks to disillusion her, she is upset. At the very end, when Lennart has rushed about trying to find postcards and discover departure times in an empty part of the airport--a scene with distinct Kafkaesque overtones--he finds the grandmother together with her childhood friend, John, a doctor who is said to be able to help people suffering from illusions and lapses. Lennart overhears his grandmother telling John that time has no significance for her--she finds days and nights equally beautiful. She is happy in her world, however it has been fashioned, and John's final words to her as they proceed to their plane are, "We have plenty of time" [39].

After this delightful story, there is a radical change of mood in "Locomotive," undoubtedly the most powerful and intense story in the volume. The narrator, who like many of Tove Jansson's characters is not named, is a loner, a man living entirely in a world of

## The Doll's House

make-believe, obsessed with what he calls the "idea" of the locomotive. He is a draughtsman who in his spare time makes colored drawings of locomotives; in his eyes, however, they are not just drawings, but an attempt to express the innermost being of the locomotive. He cuts himself off from the world around him, but in his sporadic enforced contacts with other people, his aim is always to make them betray themselves by talking and talking until they give away their most profound secrets. This he calls "the moment of the locomotive." From these "moments" he derives a--false--sense of power.

As a child, he has walked to school through the railway station each day, making up stories of trains or shipwrecks in which it is always he who has the power of life and death over others--he is the "imperator," he says. Even now, he sometimes goes to the station, and on one such visit, he meets a woman in the station restaurant. They start talking. She is in the station because she likes watching trains--and the narrator immediately interprets this innocent remark as a sign that she is also interested in the "idea" of the locomotive. He meets her again weeks later, and a "friendship" develops between them. He appoints her as his daily help, and she gradually begins to take him over in the same way as he has taken over other people in his imagination.

He becomes disenchanted when he discovers that the character with which he has endowed her in his imagination has nothing to do with reality: she is not interested in any abstract ideas but is an ordinary woman who, as she herself has said, likes watching trains. However, a relationship of some kind is struck up between them; she gains more and more power in his home, and while she is obviously trying to see to his needs and fuss over him, he feels she is devouring him. When she finally sees one of his color illustrations, her exclamation is as forthright as that of the child in Andersen's story of the emperor's new clothes: "But they are standing still." Frustrated, disillusioned, and weary, he decides "to let her die." The final section of the story tells how she persuades him to go for a weekend in Rovaniemi, and how he plans to dispose of her. It is not clear whether he does actually murder her, but in view of the number of plans he lists for getting rid of her, it can safely be assumed that the one he apparently carries out also merely takes place in the mind. He lacks the strength of purpose to kill her in reality, and the plan to dispose of her is really only another in the long series of imaginary events in which he has been the master of life and death.

In this complex story, Tove Jansson is working on two or three different levels. There is the straightforward portrayal of the narrator living in a world of his own, a world created by a neurotic, perhaps even psychotic, personality. He is interested only in machines, because of their "supreme indifference" to other people, and he is afraid of the demands people might make on him. He dislikes physical contact with people, even avoids such expressions as "to lend a hand" because they imply physical contact, and so when the Woman (whose name, Anna, he can scarcely bring himself to use) stands and holds his hand as a train comes in, she is damning herself in his eyes--though a warm <u>frisson</u> goes through him at the same time. When she puts her arms around him, the heat of her body fills him with disgust. His only contact with other people is to try to discover their secret beings, and there is a demonic urge in him to take them over and derive strength from them. However, ironically, this is precisely what he feels that the Woman is doing to him--though as it is all experienced through his eyes, we have only his rather unreliable word for it, and there is no other concrete evidence to suggest that her approaches to him are anything but those of a woman feeling growing affection for a man with whom she is seeking contact. He speaks to her, compulsively, until he has betrayed everything about himself, and the story is full of expressions indicating the extent to which he feels he has surrendered himself to her. He even dreams of her: ". . . she came closer, hopping like a black bird over the rails, she was hot and smelled of sweat and held her arms outstretched to take hold of me, and at the same time I knew that she already had me, she had the whole of me packed into her stomach, undigested and with no possibility of release" [61]. In committing these strikingly Freudian images to paper, the narrator is, of course, also betraying himself on a different level--to the reader. His jottings are often disjointed, and although for the sake of "objectivity," he tries to tell his story in the third person, he resorts to the first person as he becomes more and more emotional about what he has to tell. And as he becomes increasingly obsessed with the idea that the woman in some way has devoured him, the crisis he is undergoing is underlined by more and more frequent references to how tired he is; he often has to stop his account, sometimes in mid-sentence, and return to it later.

Very little is learned of the woman, as everything is seen through the narrator's eyes. She is the only person he has ever been interested in, but the personality he ascribes to her is one he imagines and is therefore a projection of himself. The general impression of her is that she is a very ordinary, even colorless person who is probably genuinely fond of the narrator--or at least uses him as a relief from her own loneliness.

While "Locomotive" examines a sick mind, "A Tale from Hilo, Hawaii" turns to the mind of an innocent abroad, a young hippie from America who comes to a small town in Hawaii with the preconceived notions of the ignorant foreigner. Hilo is no paradise: it is a seedy little place, with a lot of rubbish on the shore, and when Frans decides to tidy it up, he merely makes it worse than ever. He stays on, a well-intentioned but unrealistic hanger-on, properly speaking unwanted, but in a way liked by the local population. The narrator points out that unfortunately he took a liking to him--and implies that he was never paid for the board and lodging he gave him.

In contrast to "Locomotive," this is a light and humorous story in which the only sense of tragedy is that of the encroachment of modern civilization on a somewhat backward outlying area of Hawaii. However, it has serious overtones, underlined perhaps by the inability of Frans and the grandmother to communicate, as the grandmother, with her ninety-seven years, does not speak English, thus affording the narrator the opportunity of covering up for her and embarking on a series of lies to placate the young tourist. On a different level, the inability to communicate spreads to the clash of cultures, as the young hippie fails to understand the Hawaiian culture in which he finds himself. He is misunderstood and misunderstanding, and much as people like him, he is an object of gentle fun. By the end of the story, he has been accepted, but only as part of a kind of game.

"A Memory from the New Country" is a more everyday tale, drawing on the experiences of three Finnish sisters who have emigrated to the United States. The eldest of them, Johanna, has responsibility for the other two, and of these the younger, Siiri, soon shows signs of irresponsibility. She marries a good-for-nothing Italian, a small-time thief who proceeds to exploit the sisters' meager financial resources. In a final confrontation with the Italian brother-in-law, Johanna threatens him with the police if he does not go away. He leaves, and the three sisters settle down to a normal, uneventful life in their new country.

This is an uncomplicated, though scarcely light-weight story, in which more than one private world is glimpsed. The obvious one is Siiri's marriage to her Italian, a dream that could not possibly come true, an infatuation if not an obsession. However, in a way, this is counterbalanced by Johanna's own private world, as she is trying in America to maintain the Finnish quality of their lives, to create a little bit of Finland in America. Perhaps there is even a hint that a make-believe world, in this case the Finland Society of which Johanna is a member, is necessary in order to survive in alien surroundings. The third of Tove Jansson's essential themes also glimpsed is the inability of the three sisters to communicate with each other. Johanna understands the situation, but she is unable to penetrate Siiri's silence, while Maila, the middle sister, is torn between the two and is in her turn less than open with Johanna. It is an almost archetypal situation, with the eldest sister feeling her responsibility and the younger ones resenting, to varying degrees, the authority that is naturally hers.

Following her custom of varying the weight and seriousness of the stories within one volume, Tove Jansson now proceeds to a longer and more intense story, "The Strip Cartoon Artist." It would be wrong to talk of an autobiographical story, but there must be a considerable element of personal experience in it in view of Tove Jansson's own activities in this very field. Despite the American setting and the fictitious action, it is obvious that some of the atmosphere surrounding the strip cartoonist must result from an intimate knowledge of the scene.

Allington, the creator of the world-famous "Blubby" has given up his job, and his paper is desperately trying to find a successor who can continue the series without interruption. A young artist called Stein takes over the task and moves into Allington's spot in the newspaper offices. He tries to discover why Allington has given up, what has become of him, and both his and the reader's curiosity is aroused by the evasive answers he is given. In the end he discovers where Allington lives and goes to visit him. Allington talks at length about the pressures on the artist and the intellectual monotony of the job. As the conversation continues, it becomes apparent that he has suffered a nervous breakdown as a result of his work and the strain it has put on him. In the abrupt but effective ending to the story, he offers to do a few drawings for Stein if he ever needs inspiration.

Possible personal experience apart, this story puts the dilemma of the commercial artist into perspective. He has to create, whether the inspiration is there or not, and what he creates has to be good. There is no time to relax, and it is significant that on glancing in a mirror toward the end of the story, Stein notices that he is looking tired. He, like Allington before him, is living in a world apart, but it is a world created through outside pressures rather than one resulting from some twist in his own personality. Stein is a stable young man at the beginning of the story and indeed also at the end of it, but he has now seen the ravages that stress of this kind can bring about in another human being who was equally normal.

Problems of the artist are also present in "White Lady," in which three ladies of around sixty are out enjoying themselves. The general problem of ageing--as opposed to old age--is implicit in this glimpse of the three in a restaurant on an island outside Helsinki, enjoying the feeling of relaxation and looking back on their youth. Yet they have little contact with the young people they meet there, although they do try to talk to them. Ellinor, the writer, specializes in novels for young people, but she now begins to realize how little she really knows them and how little she has in common with them.

Not unlike the novel Sun City, "White Lady" portrays ageing people unable to come to terms with the age they have attained and wanting to keep in touch with younger people, but unable to do so. As in the novel, certain facets of their personalities become slightly exaggerated as they age: Regina's sentimentality, and Ellinor's love of metaphors. At the end, the shadow of death passes as the boat approaches to take them back to Helsinki, and May (like Mrs. Rubinstein in the coach in Sun City) refers to it as Charon's barge. They have all spent an evening in an artificial world, dreaming of a world that is past--if it ever existed--and in Charon's barge, they are being ferried back to reality.

"Art in Nature," which comes next, also takes place on an island. Again it is a world on its own, a world this time in which art dominates. The only person left in this open-air exhibition at night is a watchman, who lives his own life among the paintings and sculptures. He prefers the sculptures. One evening he is going his rounds and comes across a middle-aged couple having their own little barbecue, and after the inevitable reprimands, he starts talking to them about a parcel they have with them. It is an abstract painting they have bought, and they cannot agree as to what it represents. The watchman suggests that they should wrap it up artistically and hang it unopened on the wall instead of disagreeing: "That's the strange thing about art. Everyone sees in it what he can, and that's the intention" [145]. He avoids having to comment on the subject of the painting by saying that it is too dark to see it, after which he returns to his own unadorned room.

One of the shortest stories in the book, this merely hints at some of the main themes--the artist's problem in communicating with the public, the object of abstract art, and the necessity for the viewer to participate actively in understanding it. Indirectly, the question of communication between human beings is suggested, and the watchman is a clear example of someone living apart from the world of reality. However, none of the motifs is dealt with at length, and the story aims to set the mind in action rather than to provide any kind of answer to the questions it raises.

"Leading Role" continues the study of the artist's problems, in particular the need for some kind of inspiration. In "The Strip Cartoon Artist," Allington has spoken at length on the need he has felt to exploit every chance acquaintance in the quest for material: "Your own resources are dried up, and so you take everything they have and use it and exploit it, and whatever they say to you, you are wondering whether you can use it" [124]. In "Leading Role," the artist is an actress who needs to study and mentally devour an uninteresting and unsuspecting cousin in order to perfect the part she is to play. There is in Maria something of the same demonic need to absorb and live on other people's personalities as there is about Allington and the narrator in "Locomotive."

For the first time, Maria is offered the leading role in a play, but to begin with, she finds the character uninteresting. When it is pointed out to her that it is in fact very difficult to play the part of such a colorless character, she decides that her cousin Frida resembles the part so much that her best way of mastering it is to invite Frida to spend a week with her in her lonely, dismal summer house. The story is concerned with the interplay between these two characters, with Maria watching Frida's every movement and deliberately creating embarrassing silences in order to study her insecure cousin and note both her gestures and the way in which her voice dies away. When Frida finds that she can be useful about the house, her insecurity vanishes, and in order to bring it back, Maria sends for her own housekeeper to take over the work. Little does the cousin realize that on going to her room, Maria is noting her every gesture and trying to rehearse her movements in front of a mirror. The supreme irony comes when Frida fails to understand how Maria can be so considerate of her--a remark that obviously has its parallel in the play under rehearsal, where Ellen, the colorless principal figure, also fails to realize that she is being cruelly treated.

There is little sign of real contact between the two women, but toward the end Maria is overcome with what she sees as Frida's natural goodness, and although there is not sufficient warmth about her completely to efface the impression of a cold, calculating actress, a modicum of sympathy begins to emerge, and Maria decides at least to play the part of a good hostess.

Frida is a type not entirely unknown in Tove Jansson's work, the little, unattractive, and neglected person whom life is obviously passing by. The contrast between her and the calculating Maria is underlined by the scene in which the reader on the one hand sees everything through Maria's eyes and on the other realizes that Maria is consciously studying her. Sympathy is aroused for Frida for the very reason that she <u>is</u> experienced through Maria's eyes, and the use to which she is being put is very clear indeed.

"Leading Role" is an examination of artistic integrity and artistic self-sufficiency. How far can an artist create without consciously drawing on others for inspiration? The narrator in "Locomotive" can only with reservations be called an artist, but the signs are that Allington is one on his way and that Maria is at least a capable actress. Yet none of them is able to support his or her art without a deliberate and conscious exploitation of other, unsuspecting people. In different ways and to different extents, all three of these figures have a vampire-like quality, drawing their life strength from other living beings, who might then go on to praise them for their originality. One of the problems for the artist appears to be the necessity of exploiting human beings in order to communicate with--human beings.

In "Flower Child," there is no exploitation of people, but the question of human contact looms large, coupled with the problem of ageing and the changes it brings about within a person or a group of people. Flora Johansson is a svelte young thing who lives a gay life as a young girl, surrounding herself with friends of like mind. She marries an American and goes to live in the United States where she continues her spoiled and carefree life. Time passes and Flora is prevented from going to Finland by the war. Her parents die, and so does her husband. In the end she goes back to Helsinki and rejoins her former friends. All have looked forward to the reunion, but all have aged and changed, and the close contact that formerly existed is no longer to be found. After the first elation, things settle down. Memories can no longer provide the stuff for more than superficial conversation: "The close-knit circle around an all too small table presupposed an intimate contact which no longer existed" [166]. And moreover, that contact cannot be re-established.

Flora's life in Helsinki is now a lonely one. Her friends have other interests and duties--jobs, grandchildren, worries about their health--but she has nothing to live for except her own memories. And that is precisely what she does. She creates her own world of memories, imagining that she has guests, entertaining them, dismissing them when she has had enough. And she plies them with champagne, which she buys in great quantities and needs in order to keep a clear view of what is going on around her. Time begins to have little significance for her, almost as little as for the grandmother in "Time Concept," and she sleeps when she feels the need, at any time of the day: "And Flora went to sleep on her fur, and the day passed into twilight, and she woke up and drank just a little champagne, just a single glass so that she could see and experience everything the clearer" [169]. Like many of the other stories in this collection, this has an open ending, and these final words indicate the hopeless and unchanging situation in which Flora now finds herself.

"Flower Child" is the story of a "light" woman, a woman who seeks superficial enjoyment in a world of her own and is finally faced with a reality with which she cannot cope. She has never understood her husband's business, and even the luxury in which she has lived as the wife of a rich businessman has been a false world, as he has been heading for bankruptcy. She has been fêted and spoilt, has scarcely grown up, while her friends have developed in a different direction. What once united them now divides them, and the contact that was there before is there no longer. It is a tragic story of loneliness and a hunger for contact growing with the years.

The last of the stories, "The Great Journey," takes up the theme of the imaginary journey found in "Locomotive," though the story itself is very different. It tells of a triangle. Rosa is torn between her friend, Elena, and her mother. Both want to travel with her, but Rosa is tied to her mother and cannot go away with Elena, with whom a very close relationship is indicated. The mother, who has dominated Rosa, has always been promised a trip abroad, but has never managed to go on one, and now she travels in her imagination to places with exotic names such as Gafsa and Bahia. Rosa is like Frida in "Leading Role," a gentle person with a constant bad conscience even if she has done nothing to merit it. Elena tries to persuade her to break the bond that ties her so closely to her mother, but finally changes to persuading her to take the mother to the Canary Islands. What effect this will have on their relationship is left unclear. The dream world motif and the idea of the limits to understanding, this time among three people, are clearly discernible.

Taken as a whole, <u>The Doll's House</u> is a natural continuation of Tove Jansson's earlier work, a book in which she continues to examine the themes on which she has already laid so much emphasis. In all these stories, there is some character living in a dream world or a world not perceived by anyone else, a "doll's house." The extent to which they are divorced from reality varies considerably; in some cases, it is merely a constituent part of a totality, but in others it emerges, takes on a life of its own, and leads either to neurosis or psychosis or demonic fascination. There is even enough to suggest the need in people for some kind of "life dream"--perhaps related to Ibsen's "life lie"--as the basis on which to live their lives. It emerges at least as a book about people's need for some kind of dream with which to supplement the reality of a humdrum or demanding everyday life.

## *Chapter Sixteen*
# Conclusion

The line of development in Tove Jansson's work seems to be determined by the conflict between the demands placed on her from outside, as a successful children's author and cartoonist, and her own need to communicate, as an artist, on a different level. Even in the earliest of the children's books, it is possible to discern ideas and associations that may not immediately be of interest to children. They were not noticed by adults at first, and it is only with the hindsight acquired by reading a large number of her books that these themes can be seen in her early work.

As the Moomin series proceeds, the overtones become more obvious, until it is the poetry and the overtones that dominate in the final books in the series, while the fantasy characters are no longer childlike and simple but increasingly adult and complex. As this change in concept takes place, it becomes clear that the children's book is no longer a sufficient medium for the writer. She is changing, has changed, and she needs a means of expression less inhibited by the need to appeal to children. One of the consequences is an increasing preoccupation with the problems of art and inspiration, the question of artistic integrity and the role of the artist. It also may well be that she was feeling frustrated by the sheer success of her cartoon series with its constant demands for fresh inventiveness. She was, in fact, whether she liked it or not, living in a kind of Moomin world from which she had to break out. It was at this stage that she made her first move toward purely adult literature in The Sculptor's Daughter.

In this and the slightly later Summer Book, Tove Jansson still does not stray very far from the children's book. Her Moomin world is behind her, but she still writes simply, in a manner reminiscent of stories told for children, though the overtones place these books in the adult category. New themes begin to assert themselves, and in The Summer Book, old age assumes a new and important role. It is well known that children and old people often find things in common, and here Tove Jansson explores that area, seeking to define how much they share and where the limits in one particular grandmother-grandchild relationship lie. In its turn, this leads to the consideration of old age itself and the changes that affect people as they age.

These themes are again present in The Listener, in which the author's penchant for the short story takes a new turn, and they dominate in Sun City, her most ambitious examination of old age and the effects of ageing. If Miss Peabody from this novel is considered along with Sniff from the Moomin books, the implication seems to be that characteristics already present in children assert themselves in a new and uncompromising form in old people. The Doll's House then examines the intermediate stage, when personal idiosyncrasies in some people acquire a strength of their own and lead to abnormal behavior. The author now moves firmly into the area of mental disturbance, which has been close to the surface as far back as some of the stories in the Moomin books, particularly in "The Fillyjonk Who Believed in Disasters." Even there, obsessions were sensed--the hemulens' concern with collecting and arranging, the fillyjonks' passion for tidiness. What could only be hinted at there is here often expanded and made the center of a profound and often disturbing study, and these aspects of human nature are given a universal significance they could never have had when represented by hemulens and fillyjonks.

A surprising number of the characters in the adult books--and for that matter in the Moomin books--are plagued with the problem of establishing contact with others. They create a world of their own, where they live and work and from where they find it difficult to communicate with those outside, much as they may wish to do so. They are human islands, difficult of access and blown over by violent crises. Could it be that the islands and the storms in the Moomin books are themselves early symbols of this sense of isolation? There is certainly a striking number of descriptions of journeys to islands, stays on islands, and storms either at sea or on islands. They can be seen as purely descriptive and "exciting" parts of the narrative, but the adult reader might begin to suspect more.

*Conclusion* 165

Tove Jansson's work is open to many interpretations. It can be read--and will by children almost certainly be read--without interpretation. It can be seen allegorically as the depiction of Finland in the modern world or, more narrowly, of the Finland-Swedes within Finland. Or the allegory can be broadened to encompass humanity threatened by forces out of control--atomic warfare and ecological disaster--in which case it is natural for the individual to fashion a private world and seek to live in it undisturbed.

Whatever the interpretation, Tove Jansson's work is very much that of the visual artist. In the Moomin books, this is apparent from the close relationship existing between the illustrations and the text, a relationship so close that many critics have pointed out that the text can scarcely be imagined without the illustrations. The adult literature is not generally illustrated, but the visual observations are as clear as ever. Perhaps the most unusual but significant of these observations is that of the custodian in "Art in Nature," when because of a spinal defect he is forced to sit and watch the feet and legs of the people walking past and can make far-reaching deductions from his observations. It is a brief description, outstanding in its precision. Precise observation is balanced by countless lyrical descriptions of nature in all its moods, usually quite brief, but often of striking beauty, whether they be of violent storms or of tranquil moods, in which the atmosphere as well as the externals of nature are re-created.

Not only does Tove Jansson observe and understand the characters she draws, but she evinces great sympathy and forebearance toward them all, even the most difficult and apparently unattractive of them. It would be difficult if not impossible to find any of them depicted in a critical or negative light. Many of them are superficially uncomplicated beings, but often they have unplumbed depths. Signs of unexpected complications behind a placid or simple facade can be found in the later Moomin books, and the tendency becomes more pronounced in <u>Summer Book</u> and <u>Sun City</u>. To talk of the simplicity of the characters in <u>The Doll's House</u> would be a gross exaggeration; the central figures are almost all portrayed as complicated. They are often on the borderline between normality and abnormality, and some of them have crossed it.

Tove Jansson's work is not yet finished, but <u>The Doll's House</u> seems to constitute a major breakthrough in which the tensions apparent in the earlier books have been worked out and to some extent resolved. It thus comes to stand as the culmination of Tove Jansson's work so far, and perhaps points the way to yet another phase in her production.

# List of English Names with Swedish Equivalents

| | |
|---|---|
| ancestor | förfadern |
| Bob | Vifsla |
| Daddy Jones | Pappa Blomkvist |
| Edward the Booble | Dronten Edvard |
| Fillyjonk | Filifjonk |
| Gaffsie | Gafsan |
| Grandpa Grumble | Onkelskrutet |
| Groke | Mårran |
| hattifattener | hatifnat |
| hemulen | hemul |
| Hobgoblin | Trollkarl |
| Hodgkins | Frederiksen |
| Joxter | Joxaren |
| Misabel | Misan |
| Moomintroll | Mumintrollet |
| Muddler | Rådd-djuret |
| Muskrat | bisamråtten |
| Mymble | Mymla |
| Nibling | klippdass |
| Ninny | Ninni |
| Salome the Little Creep | knyttet Salome |
| Sniff | Sniff |
| Snork Maiden | Snorkfröken |
| Snufkin | Snusmumriken |
| Sorry-oo | Ynk |
| Teety-woo | Ti-ti-oo |
| Thingummy | Tofsla |
| Too-ticky | Too-ticki |
| Whomper | homsa |

# Notes and References

Page references are given in the text. Those enclosed in parentheses refer to the English translations, Puffin editions. Those in brackets refer to the original Swedish editions, and in these cases, the translations are my own.

Chapter One

1. Ulla-Stina Nilsson, "Mumindalen, vort genoplevede barndomsland," Information, 24 May 1966, p. 8.
2. Ibid.
3. Frederic and Boel Fleischer, "Tove Jansson and the Moominfamily," American Scandinavian Review, Spring 1963, p. 47.
4. Bo Carpelan, Interview, in Min väg till barnboken, ed. Bo Strömstedt (Stockholm, 1971), p. 102.
5. Ibid., pp. 97-98.
6. A similar comment is found in Tove Jansson's interview with Fleischer "Tove Jansson," p. 52.
7. Harriet Clayhill, "Drömmen om Muminhuset," Allt i Hemmet, no. 2 (1976), p. 29.
8. Lennart Utterström, "Möte med Mumin," Hufvudstadsbladet, 30 September 1973, p. 3.
9. W. Glyn Jones, "Tove Jansson. My Books and Characters," Books from Finland 11, no. 3 (1978):93.
10. Look at Finland, no. 3 (1979), p. 47.
11. Private MS.
12. Private MS.
13. Ebba Elfving, "Muminmammans värld," Damernas värld, 20-28 June 1965, p. 19.
14. Jones, "Tove Jansson," p. 96.
15. "Trygghet och skräck i barnboken," Mediernas värld, Sveriges Radio, Stockholm 1977, p. 104.
16. John Bauer, Swedish artist (1882-1918).
17. Ivar Arosenius, Swedish artist and writer (1878-1909).
18. Elsa Beskow, Swedish children's writer (1874-1953).

19. Jones, "Tove Jansson," p. 97.
20. Fleischer, "Tove Jansson," p. 49.
21. Ibid.
22. "Moomintrolls in many ways," Books from Finland, no. 3 (1980), p. 128.
23. Fleischer, "Tove Jansson," p. 53.
24. At this point, the books seem to change from what might be called children's tales to novels proper, with the development of character and the consideration of problems that rightly belong to that genre.
25. Jones, "Tove Jansson," p. 91.
26. Ibid., p. 95.
27. Zachris Topelius, Finland-Swedish author (1818-98).
28. Selma Lagerlöf, Swedish author (1858-1931).
29. Erik Axel Karlfeldt, Swedish poet (1864-1931).
30. Carpelan, Interview, in Min väg till barnboken, ed. Strömstedt, p. 100.
31. Ibid.
32. Letter, 15 June 1981.
33. Jones, "Tove Jansson," p. 95.

Chapter Three

1. Carpelan, Interview, in Min väg till barnboken, ed. Strömstedt, contains the following comment by TJ: "At first I had rather too many exotic palm trees, but now they have disappeared. I try to be factual in my account, for instance, of the passing seasons. Children are very particular about such things. The moon must rise in the right place--but of course, it can be as big as you wish. It is hardly wrong to say that I have a realistic, even naturalistic, view of my Moomin world, at least as far as milieu and natural scenery are concerned."

Chapter Four

1. The English version calls him a "hobgoblin," but I prefer to keep to the Swedish designation except in direct quotations.

Chapter Five

1. My translation. This passage, taken from pp. 12-13 of the Swedish original, has not been included in the English translation.

2. My translation. Swedish edition, p. 8.
3. My translation. Swedish edition, p. 9.

Chapter Nine

1. The significance of the lighthouse requires some consideration. According to an article in Damernas värld, 21-28 June 1965, p. 19, the lighthouse was inspired by one that TJ had visited as a child. It seems to have various symbolical interpretations: the family's changing attitude toward it goes with the transformation they themselves undergo, while in the final episode in which it is finally lit, it might be seen as a symbol of Pappa's ultimate enlightenment. It can be--and has been--seen as a virility symbol, but this seems too easy and banal to be convincing.

Chapter Twelve

1. It should be remembered that the question of representational drawings is at the center of the story entitled "Locomotive" in The Doll's House.

Chapter Thirteen

1. This watercolor is caricatured in Moominpappa at Sea in a drawing depicting Pappa sitting outside the tent in which Mamma is sleeping on her first night on the island.

# Selected Bibliography

**PRIMARY SOURCES**

1. Tove Jansson's Works in Swedish
Note: All first editions published by Schildt, except <u>Småtrollen och den stora översvämningen</u> which was published by Söderström.

<u>Småtrollen och den stora översvämningen</u>. Helsinki 1945.
<u>Kometjakten</u>. Helsinki 1946.
<u>Trollkarlens hatt</u>. Helsinki 1948. Edition quoted: Helsinki 1968.
<u>Muminpappans Bravader</u>. Helsinki 1950.
<u>Farlig Midsommar</u>. Helsinki 1954. Edition quoted: Helsinki 1969.
<u>Trollvinter</u>. Helsinki 1957. Edition quoted: Helsinki 1970.
<u>Det osynliga barnet</u>. Helsinki 1962. Edition quoted: Stockholm 1974.
<u>Pappan och havet</u>. Helsinki 1965.
<u>Kometen kommer</u>. Helsinki 1968.
<u>Sent i november</u>. Helsinki 1971. Edition quoted: Stockholm 1974.

<u>Bildhuggarens dotter</u>. Helsinki 1968. Edition quoted: Helsinki 1969.
<u>Lyssnerskan</u>. Helsinki 1971. Edition quoted: Stockholm 1973.
<u>Sommarboken</u>. Helsinki 1972.
<u>Solstaden</u>. Helsinki 1974.
<u>Dockskåpet</u>. Helsinki 1978.

2. Tove Jansson in English
Note: All first editions of the novels in translation were published by Ernest Benn. Permission to quote from the English editions of Tove Jansson's Moomin books has been given by the copyright holders, Messrs. Ernest Benn Ltd.

## Selected Bibliography

Finn Family Moomintroll. Translated by Elizabeth Portch. London 1951. Edition quoted: Puffin Books, 1980.
Comet in Moominland. Translated by Elizabeth Portch. London 1951. Edition quoted: Puffin Books, 1980.
The Exploits of Moominpappa. Translated by Thomas Warburton. London 1952. Edition quoted: Puffin Books, 1980.
Moominsummer Madness. Translated by Thomas Warburton. London 1955. Edition quoted: Puffin Books, 1979.
Moominland Midwinter. Translated by Thomas Warburton. London 1958. Edition quoted: Puffin Books, 1980.
Tales from Moomin Valley. Translated by Thomas Warburton. London 1963. Edition quoted: Puffin Books, 1980.
Moominpappa at Sea. Translated by Kingsley Hart. London 1965. Edition quoted: Puffin Books, 1980.
Moominvalley in November. Translated by Kingsley Hart. London 1971. Edition quoted: Puffin Books, 1977.
The Sculptor's Daughter. Translated by Kingsley Hart. London 1969.
The Summer Book. Translated by Thomas Neal. London 1972.
"The Monkey." Translated by W. Glyn Jones, Books from Finland 14, no. 2 (1981):62-63.
"Locomotive." Translated by W. Glyn Jones, Books from Finland 14, no. 2 (1981):64-71.

**SECONDARY SOURCES**

1. Bibliography

TARKKA, PEKKA. Suomalaisia nykykirjailijoita. Helsinki: Tammi, 1980, pp. 65-67. Two-page article in book of similar brief descriptions of major modern Finnish writers. Contains main biographical details and list of TJ's work.

2. Books

HAGEMAN, SONJA. Mummitrollbøkene. Oslo: Aschehoug, 1967. Discussion of TJ's principal characters and a chronological description of Moomin books up to Moominpappa at Sea. A little on TJ's style.
JONES, W. GLYN. Tove Jansson: Pappan och havet. Studies in Swedish Literature no. 11. Hull: Depart-

ment of Scandinavian Studies, University of Hull, 1979. An analysis of Moominpappa at Sea, dealing with main themes and aspects of the narrative. Also contains section on TJ and select bibliography.

JUTIKKALA, EINO, and PERINEN, KAUHO. A History of Finland. Espoo: Wellin & Göös, 1979. A good, fairly long history of Finland, useful for the historical background.

KLINGE, MATTI. A Brief History of Finland. Helsinki: Otava, 1981. A very short review of Finnish history by a leading historian.

STRÖMSTEDT, BO. Min väg till barnboken. Stockholm: Bonniers, 1971. A book on various authors' approach to children's writing, containing a stimulating interview with TJ by Bo Carpelan.

3. Articles

FLEISCHER, FREDERIC and BOEL. "Tove Jansson and the Moominfamily," American-Scandinavian Review, Spring 1963, pp. 47-54. Brief description of Moomin books, including interview with TJ.

JONES, W. GLYN. "Studies in Obsession. The New Art of Tove Jansson." Books from Finland 14, no. 2 (1981):60-62. Brief introduction to TJ's work, touching on some of the themes developed in the present study.

───. "Tove Jansson and the Artist's Problem," Scandinavica 22, no. 1 (May 1983). A discussion of the themes of art and the artist as seen in TJ's work.

───. "Tove Jansson. My Books and Characters." Books from Finland 14, no. 3 (1978):91-97. Lengthy interview with TJ, in which she reviews her approach to writing, her feelings about children's books, the theme of loneliness in her work, her approach to adult writing and her work as an artist.

RANHEIM, KIRSTEN. "Utviklingen i Tove Janssons muminforfatterskap," Norsk litterær årbok, 1977. A thorough study of stylistic and thematic development of TJ's Moomin books.

4. Dissertation

OMLAND, KIRSTEN. "Tryggheten og skrekken. Utviklingen i Tove Janssons Muminforfatterskap." University of Oslo, 1975. A detailed study of TJ's work, mainly the Moomin books, based on the view that the central feature is the contrast between a sense of fear and a sense of security.

# *Index*

Alice in Wonderland
  (Carroll), 9
American-Scandinavian Review, 2
Andersen, Hans Christian,
  1, 17, 39, 78, 153
Arosenius, Ivar, 9, 11

Bauer, John, 9, 109
Beskow, Elsa, 9, 11
Bradbury, Ray, 12
Burroughs, Edgar Rice, 12

Captain Grant's Children (Verne), 12
Carpelan, Bo, 3

Elfving, Ebba, 2

Far from the Madding Crowd (Hardy), 12
Fleischer, Frederic and Boel, 2
Freud, Sigmund, 42, 154

Herr Arnes Pengar
  (Lagerlöf), 12
Högfeldt, Robert, 136
Hufvudstadsbladet, 2, 10
Hunting of the Snark,
  The (Carroll), 9

Information, 1

Jansson, Lars, 7, 10
Jansson, Per Olov, 7, 10
Jansson, Signe Hammersten
  (Ham), 6, 7, 12, 128

Jansson, Tove Maria

WORKS: FOR ADULTS
Doll's House, The,
  10, 13, 59, 60, 73,
  85, 117, 118, 121,
  123, 149-62, 164,
  165, 166
Listener, The, 117-
  26, 127, 149, 164
Sculptor's Daughter,
  The, 6, 8, 9, 106-
  16, 117, 127, 137,
  163
Summer Book, The,
  9, 127-37, 163,
  165
Sun City, 129, 137,
  138-48, 151, 158,
  164, 165

WORKS: FOR CHILDREN
Comet in Moominland,
  12, 16, 17, 18, 19-
  27
Comet is Coming, The,
  19, 21, 22-27
Exploits of Moominpappa, The, 26, 38-
  47, 48, 51, 54, 75
Finn Family Moomintroll,
  26-37, 40, 46
Little Trolls and the
  Great Flood, The,
  10, 14-18, 19
Moominland Midwinter,
  11, 56-66, 67, 68,

69, 74, 75, 78, 89, 93
Moominpappa at Sea, 8, 9, 33, 41, 45, 53, 54, 58, 62, 69, 76, 79-92, 93, 94, 108, 115, 127, 134
Moominsummer Madness, 48-55, 64, 133
Moominvalley in November, 11, 41, 76, 79, 93-105, 109, 111, 113, 115
Tales from Moominvalley, 67-78
Who Shall Comfort Toffle?, 1

WORKS: INDIVIDUAL STORIES
"Art in Nature," 158, 165
"Black and White," 119
"Cedric," 76-77
"Children's Party," 118
"Doll's House, The," 150-51
"Explosion, The," 124
"Fillyjonk Who Believed in Disasters, The," 71, 121, 164
"Fir Tree, The," 77-78
"Flower Child," 160-61
"Great Journey, The," 161
"Grey Duchess, The," 122
"Hemulen Who Loved Silence, The," 73
"Invisible Child, The," 11, 74-75
"Leading Role," 158-59, 161
"Letters to an Idol," 120
"Listener, The," 117-18

"Locomotive," 70, 121, 124, 152-55
"Lucio's Friends," 124
"Memory from the New Country, A," 156
"Monkey, The," 123, 149
"Other One, The," 121
"Rain," 124
"White Lady," 157
"Wolves," 122-24
Jansson, Viktor, 6-7, 106
Jungle Book (Kipling), 12

Kant, Immanuel, 10
Krakatit (Capek), 12

Lindgren, Astrid, 1
London Evening News, 10

Mediernas värld, 9
Miller, Henry, 2

Nilsson, Ulla-Stina, 1
Nomads of the North (Curwood), 12
Ny Tid, 10

Pietilä, Tuulikki, 4, 10, 11
Pinocchio (Collodi), 12
Pippi Longstocking (Lindgren), 1
Poe, Edgar Allan, 12

Robinson Crusoe (Defoe), 38

Sea Wolf (London), 12
Spengler, Oswald, 20

Tarzan (Burroughs), 12, 37
Tati, Jacques, 2
"Thumbelina" (Andersen), 17

*Index*

Topelius, Zachris, 12
Travailleurs de la mer, Les (Hugo), 12
Typhoon (Conrad), 12

Utterström, Lennart, 5

Vildmarksdikter (Karlfeldt), 12

Winnie the Pooh (Milne), 12-13